FROM MAINE TO THE MAIN LINE

A History of
Consumers Water Company

To The Portland Public Library
in appreciation of years of
excellent service –
John Parker

FROM MAINE TO THE MAIN LINE

A History of
Consumers Water Company

By John van C. Parker

Custom Communications
Saco, Maine

Published by Custom Communications, 92 Franklin St., Saco, ME 04072
(207) 286–9295. E-mail: custom@desktoppub.com.
Web site:http://www.desktoppub.com

Library of Congress Cataloging-in-Publication Data
Parker, John van C.
From Maine to the main line: a history of the Consumers Water Company / by John
van C. Parker.
   p. cm.
   Includes bibliographical references and index.
ISBN 1-892168-06-5
1. Consumers Water Company—History. I. Title: History of the Consumers Water
Company. II. Title.
HD4464.M35 P37   2000   00–060117
363.6'1'09741—dc21

Design, Typography, and Setup
Custom Communications

Photo Credits
Dust Jacket Photos. Front: © PhotoDisc; back: courtesy of City Utilities of Springfield,
Missouri (photo by Dr. John T. Witherspoon); front flap: City Utilities of Springfield,
Missouri (photo by Michael Garoutte); back flap: courtesy of John van C. Parker.
Book Photos. Courtesy of Consumers Water Company: 3, 13; © PhotoDisc: 9; © Maine
Historical Society: 10; courtesy of Consumers Pennsylvania Water Company: 18, 120;
photos by John van C. Parker: 32, 55; © Blethen Newspapers: 41; courtesy of Han-
naford Brothers Inc.: 53 (*left*); courtesy of Central Maine Power Company: 53 (*right*);
courtesy of H.M. Payson Company: 60; courtesy of Marsha Webber: 69; courtesy of
Hannah Russell: 73; courtesy of Consumers Maine Water Company: 77; courtesy of
John White: 82; courtesy of Consumers New Jersey Water Company: 83; courtesy of
Consumers Ohio Water Company: 99 (*top and bottom*); courtesy of Consumers Illinois
Water Company; 105; courtesy of Burlington Homes of New England: 112; courtesy of
John van C. Parker: 116; © Gail Osgood: 138; courtesy of David Hastings: 144 (*left*);
courtesy of John Menario: 144 (*right*); photo by Martha Nichols: 151.

First Edition
Printed in the United States of America.
10 9 8 7 6 5 4 3 2 1

Dedication

This book is dedicated to the hundreds of loyal employees of Consumers Water Company, both past and present, without whose efforts this story would not have been possible.

Sources and Credits

There are many people who have helped me in my task. My greatest indebtedness is to my two volunteer editors. My Literary Editor was Victoria S. Poole, talented author of *Thursday's Child* (Little Brown, 1980), who did an outstanding job of cleaning up my act. My Factual Editor was John White, retired President of Consumers, whose input was vital since he knows first-hand far more of the history of the Company than I. John takes no responsibility for several items he felt were better left unsaid. The third key player was Susan Gold, a professional historian, who helped me select the illustrations and assumed all the responsibility for art work, layout, and making arrangements for publication. Next is Lorraine M. Libby, who was my Secretary and most valuable assistant at Consumers and who came out of retirement to work on this book. She is the only person I know who can talk to me on one subject while typing on another. Other sources of information, not in order of importance, are the Company corporate records from 1926 to 1963; Annual Reports to Shareholders from 1956 through 1997; Website 10-K Wizard.com; *A 100th Anniversary History of H.M. Payson & Co.* by Roger Ray; Clark T. Erwin, Corporate Communications, Central Maine Power Company; Michelle Clements, Public Relations Manager of the Portland Water District; Merrill P. Robbins, daughter of Phillips M. Payson;

Plattsmouth Memorial Library of Plattsmouth, NB; A. Vinton Lewis, retired contractor of South Portland, Maine; Marilyn A. Gaffney of Edward Jones Banking of St. Louis, MO. Stanley M. Massarelli, retired Treasurer of Ohio Water Service Company; Hannah Russell, widow of John J. Russell; Marsha Webber, daughter of Fletcher Means; Barbara J. Schultz and Kathy Pape of Philadelphia Suburban Water Company; Robert G. Liptak, Jr., current President of Consumers and scavenger for many photos; Alice Mary Pierce for genealogical research and proofreading; Peter L. Haynes, John F. Isacke, and Brian R. Mullany, respectively President, CFO, and Secretary of Consumers at the time of sale; and David Fraley, Director of Environmental Compliance, City Utilities of Springfield, Mo.

About the Author

John Parker, a native of Morristown, New Jersey, attended Phillips Exeter Academy and earned a Civil Engineering Degree from Princeton University. Following graduation, he received a commission in the Civil Engineer Corps of the United States Naval Reserve and served active duty at Kodiak, Alaska. After his military service, he worked for twelve years at the Maine Central Railroad including a leave of absence to obtain an MBA from the Amos Tuck School of Dartmouth College. In 1966 he started a twenty-six year career at Consumers Water Company, including eight as its President and CEO. He remained active in the Naval Reserve after his discharge and eventually retired as a Captain. He is now enjoying retirement in Falmouth, Maine, with his wife, Ann P. Parker. They have four children and two grandchildren.

Foreword

About a year ago, March 10, 1999, Consumers Water Company was sold to Philadelphia Suburban Company (PSC) of Bryn Mawr, Pennsylvania. For the state of Maine, it was the end of an era.

Consumers had been founded in 1926, and as it grew it increased the wealth of thousands of people, delivered high quality water service to hundreds of thousands of customers, and provided rewarding careers for hundreds of highly skilled and dedicated employees. For years it was one of only a handful of publicly traded companies both incorporated and headquartered in the state of Maine yet conducting most of its business in other states. Consumers was also, until the day it was sold, among the elite one percent of all the publicly traded companies in the United States with the longest record of uninterrupted annual increases in dividend payout to its shareholders.

A farewell dinner, hosted by the Company's President, Peter L. Haynes, was held about a month before the closing on the sale. The invited guests were all current and former officers and directors, Parent Company employees, and all the incumbent subsidiary presidents. At the dinner, Peter and retired President John W. L. White ganged up on me to request that I write a history of the Company. Who but two engineers would ask an engineer to write a book, especially one who almost flunked sophomore English? John White had asked me to tackle the task before, but I had put him off with an assertion that I had too many other things on my plate.

Yielding to their pressure, I reconsidered the matter and eventually agreed. My reasoning was thus:

(1) if I don't do it, no one else will since it is highly unlikely that the Company would hire a professional;

(2) a fair number of people in the Consumers family, i.e., employees, retirees, and many shareholders, might enjoy reading the story;

(3) the Consumers story is not an insignificant part of Maine's history, and, if it isn't recorded now, within a generation or two it will be lost and forgotten forever; and

(4) if some extra copies are published for exclusive sale by the Maine Historical Society, the Society might benefit from a fair amount of revenue. Both John White and I are Trustees of the Society.

While the research was much more time consuming than I had anticipated, the real challenge for me was to keep the book from being what most people might expect a book about a water company to be—boring. I hope I have succeeded.

—John Parker, March 2000

TABLE OF CONTENTS

Portland's Great Fire of 1866 led to the construction of a water main from Sebago Lake to the city.

CHAPTER ONE

The Entrepreneurs

Consumers Water Company was incorporated on February 25, 1926. The organizational meeting that winter Thursday was held at the Portland offices of George F. West & Son, which were in the so-called Union Mutual Building at the corner of Congress and Exchange Streets. Only four of the seven founders of the business were present, namely, Vernon F. West, Herbert Payson, Harold C. Payson, and James W. Coburn. Absent were Philip Burgess, William B. Skelton, and George F. West. But all seven men were elected directors and all seven men subscribed to one share each "at such price as the Directors may fix, upon demand of the Treasurer." The original Bylaws authorized a total of 10,000 shares.

The expressed purposes of the new corporation were extremely broad. The key provisions focused on acquiring, owning, and selling various types of securities, exercising whatever rights that might go with those securities (including whatever lawful acts might preserve or enhance their value), and entering into contracts "for any lawful purpose whatever." Conspicuously absent in the lengthy paragraph was any mention of water; but the name of the company was to be Consumers Water Company. Besides the authorization of 10,000 shares of common stock, the Bylaws also provided for the issuance of 1,000 shares of First Preferred Stock and 2,000 shares of Preferred Stock.

Who were these seven men and why did they decide to found a water utility company? Six of them were already intimately involved with the water utility industry, including owning, directly or indirectly, and wholly or in part, numerous water utility companies. The seventh, William Skelton, brought to the team both extensive experience in the utility industry, primarily power, and outstanding legal expertise. One source claims that the idea of the company came from Phil Burgess and Vernon West as they rode together on a train, most likely to visit the water utility of a common destination. The economy was roaring and there was much to be gained through the pooling of interests and a broad spectrum of technical expertise.

Phil Burgess was a senior partner in the consulting engineering firm of Burgess and Niple located in Columbus, Ohio. That firm specialized in the design and valuation of water utilities. Through his firm's associations, Mr. Burgess may have gained an interest in a few water companies and definitely had an excellent knowledge of what companies might be available for purchase and the appropriate contacts.

George F. West and his son, Vernon F. West, were the owners and principal officers of George F. West & Son. That Maine corporation was primarily a water utility construction company. Its roots go back to George P. Wescott of Portland who was engaged in the same business. At some point George Wescott invited his nephew, George F. West, to join him in the business. Eventually, after Mr. Wescott had either died or retired and George's son, Vernon, had joined the business, the two Wests incorporated as George F. West & Son.

*Vernon F. West,
Consumers' first and
longest serving President*

Among other projects, George Wescott, in 1884, contracted to build the Biddeford and Saco Water Company. The consideration for that contract was $15,000 of common stock and $10,000 of that water company's first-mortgage bonds. In those days, and well into the early years of Consumers Water Company, it was not uncommon to contract for paper rather than cash. Thus evolved the fairly wide water utility holdings of George F. West & Son, H.M. Payson & Co. and Burgess and Niple. George Wescott, and subsequently George F. West & Son, for many years contracted to operate Biddeford and Saco Water Company.

James W. Coburn was part of the group because of his involvement with George F. West & Son. Mr. Coburn was Vernon West's right-hand man, and, after the incorporation of Consumers, was Treasurer and Clerk of both George F. West & Son and Consumers Water Company. It appears that during his tenure with George F. West & Son, he, too, had gained a minor interest in a few water utilities.

Both Herbert Payson and Harold C. Payson were partners in H.M. Payson & Company, also of Portland, Maine.

Henry Martyn Payson founded that company in 1854 after returning home from the California Gold Rush. There he had worked with his mind rather than a pick or a pan. He had engaged in the buying and selling of gold and made many contacts in the financial community. He was confident he could make a comfortable living in Portland dealing in stocks and bonds as well as gold. Along the way, he became involved with what was then called the Portland Water Company. During the Great Fire of July 4, 1866, it became painfully obvious that the supply of water on or near the Portland peninsula was totally inadequate for the need. In response, on Thanksgiving Day, 1869, water began to flow through a new main from Sebago Lake to Portland. However, because of substandard construction and design, as well as a heavy debt burden, the flow of both water and revenues was inadequate. After the enterprise went through bankruptcy twice, Henry M. became both a director and financial consultant of the struggling water utility. For H.M. Payson this was the start of a long relationship with not just that water company but also the entire industry.

A few years later, in 1879, H.M. Payson & Company received a real shot in the arm when Henry's nephew, Charles H. Payson, joined the business. Both energetic and shrewd, Charles elected to focus primarily on the water utility business. In 1886, along with two gentlemen from Pittsburgh and others, Charles founded the American Water Works and Guarantee Company, which was to engage in the building and development of water companies. Two years later, Charles, along with George F. Thurston and George S. Payson, all of the partners of H.M. Payson at that time, formed American Water Supply Company which concentrated on owning and operating water utilities. Neither company should be confused with the current leader of the water utility industry, American Water Works Company. Over the years, American Water Supply owned and operated from its Portland office water utilities from New Hampshire to Colorado. It was clearly a dress rehearsal for Consumers Water Company. Through its activities with both American companies and a multitude of underwritings for other companies as well, H.M. Payson & Company soon gained both national and international recognition and was widely known as "The Water Bond House." American Water Supply Company endured through 1929. Why, in 1926, the Paysons elected to form Consumers Water Company with a mission similar to American's is not clear unless it was to join forces with the West family. During the overlap, American was gradually liquidated with most, but not all, of its holdings transferred to Consumers. H.M. Payson's leadership in the financial end of the water business endured through the Depression. By then, the construction of water utilities, which had peaked near the turn of the century, had abated significantly but refinancings and the need to finance improvements and expansions still provided the bread and butter business for H.M. Payson & Company.

The seventh original owner and director was William B. Skelton of Lewiston, Maine. Consumers Water Company was not a big factor in Mr. Skelton's busy life, but Consumers was fortunate to have him on board as it was being organized. His obituary, published in February 1964, (age 92) is overwhelming. He was obviously a man of tremendous energy, expertise, and integrity. Early in his career he was active in both his legal profession and politics. During those years, he served as Banking Commissioner for the state of Maine and later as Chairman of the state's first

Public Utility Commission. Upon leaving the PUC, he became involved with Central Maine Power Company, eventually serving as Chairman of that board. Concurrent with his CMP service, he participated in the foundation of both Consumers Water Company and New England Public Service Company in 1926. For NEPSCO, Mr. Skelton was Vice President as well as one of the original directors. He eventually served as President of NEPSCO from 1942 to its liquidation in 1953. NEPSCO was more than a multi-state public utility holding company; it also controlled various industrial companies including textile mills at three Maine locations and two Maine paper mills that are still active. It appears that most, if not all, of the documents involving the formation of Consumers Water Company, as well as its numerous and involved financings and acquisitions from 1926 to 1931, were the product of his own work or prepared under his direction. How Mr. Skelton squeezed that into his already busy schedule is difficult to comprehend.

The original directors, who may appropriately be called the seven entrepreneurs, had various lengths of service on the board. First to step down was Herbert Payson who was replaced in 1930 by another H.M. Payson partner, Phillips M. Payson. Phillips was a son of Charles H. In 1932 William Skelton declined re-election. Eleven years later George F. West died. After twenty-nine years of service, Philip Burgess stepped down in 1955. James Coburn terminated both his board service and his position as Treasurer and Clerk in 1957. The longest board terms of the original seven were those of Vernon F. West and Harold C. Payson, both of whom stepped aside in 1963 after thirty-seven years of service. But the very last to leave the board was William Skelton since he rejoined the board in 1951 and was still serving when he died in 1964.

At the Company's first board meeting, Vernon West was elected President, Harold C. Payson Vice President, and James W. Coburn Treasurer and Clerk. Vernon West remained President for twenty-five years, longer than any of his successors. In 1951 Harold Payson assumed the presidency and held that office until 1957 when he retired. Along with James Coburn, he had been an officer of the Company for thirty-one years.

Shenango Valley's "new" office building in 1929. As with many other structures throughout the Consumers system, the building was designed by Portland architect John P. Thomas.

CHAPTER TWO

Building a Portfolio

On February 26, the day after Consumers was formed, a few might have thought that Consumers was a going concern. It was duly incorporated with a set of bylaws, there were seven shareholders, the Company had a board of directors, and there was a slate of officers in place. However, in reality, and quite literally, it was a paper tiger. It had no office, no employees, and no assets except, at the most, $7 in its treasury. But the tiger did have claws and it knew how to use them. The team of officers and directors was a formidable collection of all the avenues of expertise necessary to become a viable water utility holding company.

For an office, the Company immediately set up shop in the offices of George F. West & Son in the Union Mutual building at 120 Exchange Street, across the street from the Portland Newspaper building. There is no documentation as to when the Company established a payroll, but at its annual meeting in January 1927, it did establish salaries for Philip Burgess "Consulting Engineer" and Herman Burgi, Jr., "Engineer," as well as the original three officers, Vernon West, Harold Payson and James Coburn. Surely, until clerical help was added, the Company utilized the office staff of George F. West & Son. It is assumed Consumers compensated that firm for the services rendered and a percentage of the office rent. It is well known that the two companies shared a common telephone line, and, until the early 1950's, the phone was answered, "Mr. West's Office" without any mention of Consumers Water Company.

As for meeting its early day-to-day expenses, the Company must have built up significant accounts payable, primarily to George West & Son and, to a lesser extent, to H.M. Payson & Co. For legal and engineering services, the Company compensated William Skelton and Philip Burgess (Burgess and Niple) by the issuance of common shares.[1] In 1926, four Paysons, James Coburn, and George F. West & Son also accumulated common shares, but it is assumed that all of those shares were issued as consideration for water utilities purchased.

The first company purchased was the **Penobscot County Water Company**, a Maine corporation. That company was jointly owned by George F. West & Son and H.M. Payson & Company, and the consideration was 806 shares of $100 Preferred Stock and 2,500 shares of Common Stock. That transaction was approved on April 1, 1926, less than five weeks after the formation of the Company. In a competitive environment, such a transaction would normally take months, if not years, to consummate, but this was an inside deal. Since all the directors were also all the shareholders, and the vote was unanimous, there is

---

[1] One reliable source believes that the 750 shares issued to Mr. Skelton were in lieu of $500 cash. Through stock dividends and splits those shares eventually grew to 155,580 shares for Mr. Skelton's many descendants, and if all were held to the sale of

nothing the matter with that. The second purchase was arranged less than a month later but was significantly more complicated. This was for what was to become **Shenango Valley Water Company** of Sharon, Pennsylvania. Sharon is a steel town adjacent to the Ohio border.

What the Company purchased was Sharon Water Works, which had two subsidiaries, the South Sharon Water Company and the Wheatland Water Company, all interconnected. It appears that H.M. Payson & Company was a minority shareholder of Sharon, and the primary shareholders wanted cash. The total cost was to be $650,000, and Consumers did not have the resources to raise such a sum. To finance the acquisition, Consumers issued to H.M. Payson & Company $500,000 of collateral trust bonds, $100,000 of First Preferred Capital Stock, and $110,000 in cash. That adds up to $710,000, and presumably the extra $60,000 was consideration to H.M. Payson for finding and closing the transaction as well as endorsing the paper issued. How much of that paper H.M. Payson kept and how much they sold to the general public is not known, but it appears that most was sold. Besides the $60,000 kicker, Consumers was forced to pledge all of the stock of both Penobscot County Water Company and Sharon Water Works.

Within a few months of incorporation and without issuing common stock to the general public, Consumers had pulled off a $650,000 cash purchase. The arrangements, however, tied the Company into a fairly tight knot. But there was a plan to loosen the bonds, and within eight months the Company did just that. The first step was to have a general valuation of the three Pennsylvania companies. The valuation, performed by Burgess & Niple, was based on "reconstruction new less observed depreciation"

the Company they would have been worth just under $5 million. As Mark Twain once said, "Thrift is a wonderful virtue, especially in an ancestor."

(RCNLD) rather than original cost less booked depreciation, which was the basis for the balance sheets of the utilities as acquired. While the final figure of the valuation is not known, it had to be somewhere in the area of $1,666,000. That is because after completing the second step, which was to merge the three little companies into a new corporation named Shenango Valley Water Company, Shenango proceeded to issue $1 million of First Mortgage Bonds. First Mortgage Bonds are normally available only up to 60% or 65% of net plant. One million dollars was enough to pay off the $342,000 of First Mortgage Bonds of the Sharon Water Works, and the $650,000 paid for the common stock of that company. By that process, Consumers got back almost all the money it paid for the stock and transferred the indebtedness from Consumers to its wholly owned subsidiary. On top of that, Consumers had a subsidiary with a rate base about two-thirds greater than when they bought it.

Meanwhile, another potential acquisition was considered by the board at its meeting of May 8, 1926. Vernon West and Harold Payson were authorized to negotiate for the purchase of not less than 60% of the stock of the Bristol and Warren Water Works (of Rhode Island). A purchase was never consummated.

Before the end of July, however, the President asked the board for approval to purchase all of the common stock of **Beaver Valley Water Company** of Beaver Falls, Pennsylvania. It is assumed that Phil Burgess led the Company to this acquisition as he performed a physical valuation to assist the Company in evaluating the common stock. The RCNLD amounted to a little over $2,000,000, which equated to a "minimum value" of $800,000 for the common stock. The officers of the Company were authorized to purchase said stock for not more than $600,000. In actuality, a down payment had already been made on almost 90% of the stock at that price. The board also authorized the Company to arrange whatever credit terms might be required for the cash purchase, including authorization to pay H.M. Payson & Company and George F. West & Son 1% of the liability incurred each year in consideration of their endorsements. Not far from Sharon, Beaver Valley's asset values may well have been adjusted in a manner similar to Shenango Valley's.

Less than a month later, at a special board meeting, the officers were authorized to purchase all the outstanding common stock of Northern Illinois Water Company for $129,000. Northern Illinois is not to be confused with the current Northern Illinois Water Company owned by Continental Water Company. Consumers quickly changed the name of its Illinois acquisition to **Kankakee Water Company**. The purchase of Northern Illinois Water Company, from American Water Supply Co., was accomplished entirely by the issuance of 7% Preferred Stock at par.

At the same September meeting, the Company was authorized to purchase "not less than 1,800 shares of the common capital stock of the **Delaware** (Ohio) **Water Company** at $65 per share" to be paid with additional 7% Preferred Stock issued at par. That amounts to $117,000, but it is not clear how much debt came with the company. A physical valuation by Director Burgess placed the fair value at $555,000.

Shortly thereafter, Consumers pledged the common stock of both Beaver Valley and Kankakee Water Company to its outstanding collateral trust bonds in order to gain a release of the Sharon stock so that the merger and refinancing of Shenango Valley Water Company, already cited, could be effected. Once the refinancing was completed, the "Shenango bonds" issued by Consumers might have been paid off, but the Company elected to leave them outstanding in order to provide funds for other purposes, be they further acquisitions or capital improvements.

At a board meeting in August 1927, the Company was authorized to purchase all of the shares of **Williamsport** (Pennsylvania) **Water Company**, which apparently was accomplished. However, Williamsport was taken by the Town only two years later. One source indicates Consumers netted a gain of some $39,000 on the sale.

In 1928 the Company purchased, apparently for cash, the **Plattsmouth** (Nebraska) **Water Company** for $36,000 and the **York Shore Water Company** for $135,750. The latter company is a portion of what is now the York Water District in southern Maine. In 1928 the Company also sold Penobscot County Water Company for $370,760 of cash. Since the sale was to an individual, it is not known why the Company agreed to sell. The Company did book a gain of approximately $261,000 and awarded to four non-officer employees bonuses aggregating $1,500.

There were no acquisitions in 1929 although the Company did submit a bid of $290,000 for Dedham (Massachusetts) Water Company.

In 1930, however, the Company was more successful in its efforts to expand. Before that flurry of activity, at its annual meeting in January, the Company declared its first common stock dividend of $5 per share on the 10,000 shares outstanding, to be followed immediately by a 9 for 1 stock dividend, thereby increasing the number of shares outstanding to 100,000. In spite of the stock market crash three months earlier, the directors were apparently optimistic about the Company's future.

One might reasonably ask where the money was coming from to finance acquisitions for cash and a common stock dividend, not to mention the ongoing cash dividends on $500,000 of Preferred Stock outstanding and ongoing salaries and various office expenses. Gains on property sales have already been cited. More important, presumably the subsidiary companies were operating profitably, albeit even then the rates of investor-owned water utilities were regulated by state commissions. There was, however, an even more lucrative source of income to the parent company in those times. Consumers entered into management contracts with each of its subsidiaries whereby the Parent would provide:

(1) executive,

(2) supervisory,

(3) accounting and auditing,

(4) purchasing, and

(5) legal services.

The charges for such services varied from company to company but normally amounted to 3% or 4% of the subsidiary's operating revenue. It is highly unlikely that the parent company's cost for such services were as high as the fees received and, thus, they were a significant source of positive cash flow.

On top of the management services, the parent company also provided construction services consisting of:

(1) consulting,

(2) engineering, and

(3) purchasing.

For those services the Parent was paid a mark-up of 10% on everything except work performed by outside contractors, for which there was a mark-up of 5%.

In today's world, neither of those arrangements would

be acceptable to a state PUC. Rather, parent charges to its subsidiaries are always suspect in the regulatory process, and it is the exception rather than the rule that a holding company can collect even the full cost of its services to its subsidiaries.

As the year 1930 progressed, the number of shares authorized was increased from 100,000 to 102,000 and later to 104,000. Of course, a 9 for 1 stock split does not make anyone richer, and surely the motive for the split was for psychological purposes in later negotiations for acquisitions utilizing the Company's common stock. As it turned out, the vast majority of the common shareholders of a major acquisition later that year received less than ten (10) of the diluted shares of Consumers. In June of 1930, the officers were authorized to tender for the outstanding stock of **Freeport Water Company**, exchanging 3.81284 shares of Consumers for each Freeport share. The Company also offered 0.5229 shares of Consumers for each share of **Winterport Water Company**. Imagine what the exchange ratios for those two Maine companies would have been had the Company not declared its 9 for 1 stock dividend. At the same meeting, the Company also authorized the exchange of 508 shares of Consumers, plus notes payable aggregating $48,000, for all of the outstanding shares of **Hudson** (New Hampshire) **Water Company**, which was owned by Harold C. Payson and Phillips M. Payson. Title to Hudson had recently been passed to the two Paysons as American Water Supply was liquidated. Each of those three acquisitions was consummated as anticipated.

On October 6, 1930, a special stockholders meeting was called for the purposes of gaining approval for the largest acquisition for the Company to date. At that meeting, stockholders approved a tender offer for "all, or not less than 90%, of the outstanding 8,000 shares" of the common stock of **Springfield City** (Missouri) **Water Company**. The consideration for each Springfield share would be $100 of Consumers 5½%, 40-year debenture bonds plus one-fifth of a common share of Consumers, fractional shares to be adjusted in cash. If fully subscribed, Consumers would issue $800,000 in debentures plus 1,600 common shares. A little over 93% of the Springfield stock was tendered, and, thus, the acquisition was consummated before year-end.

On the positive side, Springfield increased the size of the Company significantly, thus enhancing its ability to generate cash from earnings, management fees, and construction fees. On the other hand, overnight the Company had almost $750,000 of additional debentures to service. The number of shares outstanding increased by less than 1.5%, but the number of shareholders increased from fourteen to well more than ten times that amount. While control was by no means threatened, the affairs of the Company could no longer be handled like a cozy family venture.

Nevertheless, the directors must have felt happy about the Springfield acquisition. At the directors' meeting following the annual meeting in January 1931, a 2 for 1 stock split was declared (in the form of a stock dividend), and a cash dividend of $0.25 per share after the stock split. This was a nice way to introduce some 150 new shareholders to the Company but, as it turned out, that was the last cash dividend they would see for the next twenty-four years.

In May of 1931, the Company closed on the purchase of **Roanoke** (Virginia) **Water Works Company** for $500,000 cash. That was an international affair in that the closing was held in Montreal, Canada, and at the closing 1,000 shares of First Preferred Stock of Roanoke were delivered to Compania San Pedro, a corporation of the Republic of Panama. Presumably the sale of Roanoke preferred stock reduced the net cash outlay by Consumers.

Roanoke was the last acquisition of the Company until 1959. In a little over five years, the seven entrepreneurs had created a water utility holding company with ten subsidiaries in seven states. (By 1931, Penobscot County, Williamsport, and York Shore had all been sold.) The Company's assets totaled over $22 million. The common shareholder interest was over $4.5 million, of which the founding seven owned, directly or indirectly, almost 75%; they actually controlled almost 90%. Admittedly, some of that value came from stock received for utilities sold to the new holding company, but the vast majority of it came from favorable acquisitions from third parties, creative financing, and lucrative management contracts.

On the other hand, the Company was highly leveraged and, unknown to the seven entrepreneurs, the country was less than two years into a depression that would endure for ten years. By current standards, the debt ratio was not excessive, approximately 61%. But there was a heavy layer of preferred stock, some 16%, making the common equity interest only 23%. Given the eventual duration and depth of the Depression, a bet on the Company's survival would not be particularly attractive.

CHAPTER THREE

Surviving the Depression

Consumers did survive the Depression, but the survival was not without some fancy footwork to ward off the Company's creditors.

It is quite obvious that, as was common in the early years of the Depression, the directors did not correctly anticipate its eventual depth or duration. Had they been more clairvoyant, they probably would not have leveraged the acquisition of Springfield with such a large issuance of unsecured debentures and so little common stock. Neither would they have taken two other steps already cited that further compounded that error. The first was the 2 for 1 stock dividend followed by a $0.25 per share cash dividend less than two months after the Springfield acquisition. The second was the purchase of Roanoke Water Company for cash which further increased the indebtedness of the Company. How different the circumstances would be only twelve months later.

Certainly the directors were not oblivious to the toll the Depression was taking on many, if not all, businesses. It may be that they felt the water utility industry would be depression-proof. It is true that virtually no industry would be able to do any better during a depression. In January 1930, less than three months after the Stock Market Crash, Vernon West asked the board to allow the Company to enter into a most unusual contract with Frank Rumery, owner and president of the Dartmouth Real Estate Company of Portland. It hardly seems possible that a company could be a casualty of the Depression so fast, but Dartmouth was highly leveraged and almost half of Dartmouth's real estate portfolio was automobile dealerships on Forest Avenue. In the months following the crash virtually no one was buying automobiles, and almost immediately those tenants had no cash flow to pay rent. Other tenants were surely also beginning to have troubles. Those circumstances rendered Dartmouth unable to make the monthly payments on its mortgages.

Mr. West was a good friend of Frank Rumery, and he came up with a scheme to help Mr. Rumery salvage his business. The essence of the plan was for Mr. Rumery to surrender 50% of his Dartmouth common stock to Consumers with an option to repurchase the stock for $50,000 up to January 1, 1932, and $113,500 up to January 1, 1940, but only after all unsecured loans, including loans to come from Consumers, had been paid in full. In exchange for receiving 50% of Dartmouth's stock, Consumers agreed to advance Dartmouth the necessary funds to continue servicing its debts. This was a significant contract for Consumers since the Depression lasted much longer than anyone anticipated and Mr. Rumery was, therefore, never able to exercise his recapture options. Eventually, however, all of Dartmouth's short-term debts were paid off, or forgiven, the net result of which was that Consumers owned 50% of that company with zero investment.

One interesting detail of the 1930 contract between Frank Rumery, "hereinafter called Rumery," and Consumers Water Company was that the water company was not "hereinafter called Consumers." Rather, it was "hereinafter called West." The arrangement was clearly one between Vernon West and Frank Rumery, but Vernon elected to use Consumers as his vehicle. That twist turned out to be most fortunate for Consumers.

By the time of the 1932 annual meeting of shareholders held in February, the Company had moved from the Union Mutual building to the fourth floor of 95 Exchange Street, above H.M. Payson & Company. Whether that move was an attempt to reduce the Company's office expense or a favor to H.M. Payson & Company, which owned the building, or a combination of both, is not known. The minutes of a directors' meeting a few days later include mention of a lengthy discussion on "the matter of further economies and construction expenditures." A month later at another meeting, the minutes cite a full discussion concerning the Company's finances and a need "to meet its obligations." That discussion was followed by a vote to reduce by 10% the salaries and wages of all officers and employees of Consumers and its subsidiaries who were receiving more than $20 per week, with the exception of Kankakee Water Company employees. By June of 1932, the preferred stockholders were advised that their dividends would be suspended.

A year later, financial conditions had deteriorated further. In March of 1933, holders of the $800,000 of Consumers unsecured debentures were advised that "Due to the present abnormal conditions, there will be a delay in

In 1932 Consumers moved to the fourth floor of this building, 93–95 Exchange Street, which was owned by H.M. Payson Co., the occupants of the first floor. In 1974 H.M. Payson Co. sold the building when the Dartmouth Co. purchased the former Canal Bank Building at 188 Middle Street. Dartmouth immediately converted the bank building to the first business condominium in the state of Maine, sold the first floor to H.M. Payson Co. and leased the second floor to Consumers. By coincidence, 188 Middle Street is another building designed by John P. Thomas.

the payment of the interest on the above-mentioned bonds due April 1, 1933." The Company was, however, still meeting its payments on the $500,000 of the Company's First Collateral Mortgage Gold Bonds.

Meanwhile, the Company was having trouble generating sufficient revenue in at least one of its subsidiaries. The utility law in the state of Ohio was, and still is, unique in that rates may be set by local municipalities, normally following negotiations between the municipality and the utility. Because of the financial circumstances, the city of Delaware decided that its water rates should be reduced, a move which the Company vehemently opposed. Eventually, with no agreement reached, the city passed an ordinance reducing the rates. The Company refused to reduce the rates but, because of the conflict, was forced to post a bond, thus guaranteeing a refund to the ratepayers should, on appeal, the Public Utility Commission of Ohio not sustain the Company's position.

In September 1933, the Company's debenture holders were advised that the coupons due April 1, 1933, could be surrendered for payment, but that there were not sufficient funds for payment of the October 1 coupons. Consumers was actually operating in the black, and the real problem was that, in spite of the Depression, there continued to be modest needs for water main extensions and plant improvements, the funds for which were simply unavailable on reasonable terms. Thus, rather than stonewalling customer needs or accepting outrageous bank terms, the Company elected to defer payments on its debentures. The risk, however, was that should 25% of the debenture bondholders elect to foreclose on the Company, then more serious consequences could develop. Meanwhile, dividends on the preferred stock were suspended, but the gold bonds continued to be serviced. The preferred shareholders had no rights to foreclose, but they were accumulating "deferred dividends due" which would have to be paid before a dividend could be paid on the common shares. The Company was concurrently having problems with over $1,000,000 of short-term bank notes payable, over $300,000 of which were at the parent company level. While virtually all the various banks were anxious to have their notes paid off when due, they had little choice but to extend the principal payments rather than collapse the house of cards.

Eventually, in July 1934, following extensive negotiations with both the banks and the trustee of the unsecured debentures, the Company notified the debenture holders that it had developed a plan which, if approved by the debenture holders, would place the Company on more solid footing and, in fact, improve the dubious market value of the debentures. Until conditions improved, the parties to the proposed plan would be affected as follows:

1. Interest on the debentures would be reduced from 5½% to 4% with scrip being issued with each cash payment equal to the difference. The scrip would be paid off (without further interest) when the financial circumstances of the Company improved and certainly before dividends could be paid on either the preferred or common stock.

2. All bank notes would be extended for five years and receive interest at a 4% rate. In addition, the notes would receive each year a reduction in the balance outstanding of 2% and be paid off in full before the scrip on the debentures could be paid.

3. Consumers would enjoy a significantly reduced debt service requirement at a level projected to be attainable unless conditions deteriorated further.

The plan required a 75% favorable vote to ensure that 25% of the debenture holders would not precipitate a foreclosure. The 75% requirement was realized with ample leeway.

The following March, in 1935, the Company issued a report to all of its security holders. In spite of increased revenues for the first time in three years, the overall report was negative. Further, the Company's attitude toward Franklin Roosevelt's New Deal and other government activities was quite evident. The report included the following comment: "However, with the additional Government, State and local taxes and higher costs incident to NRA and other restrictive legislation, only a small part of the new revenue was saved for the net income. With the further possibility of more rather than less government and Commission interference in the operation of utilities, your officers can look only with apprehension to the future unless the present governmental attitude toward business, and particularly utilities, is changed." Incident to that, the Company had recently been forced to write off the cost of combating the application of the city of Springfield to the U.S. Government for a "PWA loan for the building of a competing water plant." Also draining the Company's funds were a new capital stock tax and an excess profits tax imposed under the Revenue Acts of 1935 and 1936. In connection with the former, the Company voted to report the value of its capital stock at $1,500,000. The law allowed each company to declare its own value irrespective of book value or market value. The directors went on to declare that its capital stock valuation "does not represent the fair cash value, the book value, nor the market value of its stock." Presumably, the higher the declared value, the greater the tax, but there must have been some consideration of a reasonable declaration to avoid a government reversal.

Meanwhile, the rate dispute between the Company and the city of Delaware, Ohio, did not abate. The outcome was that in October 1936, the Company agreed to sell that water system to the city for $560,000. The sale, which was consummated by year-end, resulted in an after-tax profit of some $60,000. The banks holding the short-term notes outstanding agreed to have 50% of the net proceeds utilized to pay off notes and the other 50% utilized to purchase from H.M. Payson & Company notes it held from Roanoke Water Works.

There were other financial improvements during 1936. The outstanding bonds and three-year 6½% notes of Springfield City Water Company were refinanced at 4%, and the 5% Shenango Valley Water Company bonds were also refinanced at 4%. The new bond issues were twenty and twenty-five years, respectively. With increased revenues and virtually static expenses, the Company's net income increased from $93,000 in 1935 to $155,000 in 1936. In light of those circumstances, it was voted at the organizational meeting the following year to restore one-half of the pay cuts that had been imposed on the officers of the Company in 1932. Also noteworthy is the salary increase for Fletcher W. Means, Assistant Treasurer, from $50 per month to $80 per month. Fletcher, a younger cousin of Vernon West, would eventually become the third President of the Company.

The 1936 financial improvements notwithstanding, in 1937 the Company continued to experience extremely tight financial circumstances. Board minutes reflect a continuing careful scrutiny of cash flow and notes payable. The most difficult financial circumstances appeared to be at Springfield City Water Company where a major expansion of that utility's water treatment plant was underway. The 1937 minutes also reflect efforts by both the city of Roanoke, Virginia, and the city of Springfield, Missouri, to purchase their respective water utilities.

The sale of Roanoke Water Works, under the threat of condemnation by the city, progressed quickly. On April 30, 1938, the city of Roanoke paid into the Virginia courts approximately $4,600,000 and took over the operation of the Roanoke Water Works Company. That sum should not be construed as the final consideration for the sale. Those funds, however, were subsequently released piecemeal, some utilized to retire Roanoke Water Works bonds and notes and most of the balance paid to Consumers in increments through 1938 and most of 1939. By mid-1938, funds from the sale were accumulating in the parent company's treasury.

On July 1 the board approved a rather unique utilization of the $200,000 on hand. The plan was quite similar to a silent Dutch auction, if there is such a thing. All the holders of the parent company $5\frac{1}{2}\%$ debentures were advised that the Company had cash on hand from the sale of Roanoke and that the Company would purchase a limited amount of the outstanding debentures. The holders were requested to post on a form provided by the Company the price at which they were willing to sell. Obviously, those tendering at lower prices would have their tenders accepted, and the higher prices would not be accepted. Interest, which by agreement was at only 4%, would be accrued and paid up to the date of sale. The bondholders were advised that the debentures had been recently selling in a range between 40% and 50% of their face value. The Company received offers from ninety bondholders at prices that varied from 44% of face value to 100% of face value. It eventually purchased, from sixty-six bondholders, $151,300 face value bonds for $92,353 at prices that ranged from 44% to 75% with an average cost of 61%. While such an approach to the retirement of outstanding bonds would be highly unusual in today's environment, this author was informally advised that there is nothing in current SEC regulations to prevent such an approach. It should be noted that the Company was able to retire less than half the amount of bonds contemplated when the offering was made.

In 1938 and 1939 negotiations between the Company

and the city of Springfield continued. In 1939 the parties agreed to appoint three engineers to submit a valuation for the property of Springfield City Water Company.

In November 1939, the Company made another solicitation to retire its outstanding indebtedness, this time to the holders of both the 5½% debentures and the holders of the Company's first collateral, 6% bonds. Once again, it was a Dutch auction approach. On this go-around, the Company accepted tenders up to a price of 94% for the 6% collateral bonds and a price of 90% for the 5½% debentures. A total of approximately $62,000 of outstanding bonds was thereby retired. In the meantime, besides that second formal solicitation, the Company was actively purchasing its own bonds in the open market as they became available. Eventually, in early 1940, the Company elected to redeem, at a 2% premium pursuant to the terms of the indenture, $115,000 of its Series A, 6% mortgage bonds. The Company's report for the year 1939 summarizes the outcome of the Roanoke condemnation. "The amount received from the sale of Roanoke Water Works Company to the city of Roanoke was not satisfactory as the price realized was substantially less than the Company's investment therein. However, through purchase in the open market of the Consumers Water Company 5½% debentures and its first collateral mortgage 6% gold bonds, Series 'A,' at less than par, $474,800 of these securities were retired, thus enabling the Company to effect in interest savings practically what it would have received in earnings from the operation of the Roanoke Water Works Company during its ownership."

Another source, however, indicates that Consumers realized a $320,565 profit on the sale of Roanoke. Which source was correct? Both were! Here we're dealing with

semantics. Normally, in a parent company report to shareholders, "Company" means the parent company. But in the
1939 report, "less than the Company's investment therein"
referred to Roanoke Water Works' investment in water utility plant. (The company was not sold, only the utility
plant.)

After surely objecting vehemently and under oath at
the condemnation hearings about consideration less than
book value, Consumers was not about to state publicly that
it made a profit on the sale. Condemnation statutes call for
"fair value" awards. Normally a condemnation settlement
results in a sale well above book value, primarily because a
replacement of the assets taken, less an allowance for
"observed depreciation" would cost more than the book
value (original cost less book depreciation) of the assets.
But, in 1938 the Virginia court undoubtedly reasoned that
the prices of everything, including water utilities, were
depressed and a fair market value would be less than book
value.

The $320,565 profit represents that portion of the con-
demnation award that was left after paying off all of
Roanoke's debts and other obligations, less what Consumers paid for the Roanoke stock, less a capital gains tax.
Consumers had purchased the stock in 1931 at a significant
discount.

The 1939 report also summarized the Springfield situation. "Springfield City Water Company, a subsidiary of this
Company, is completing during 1940 the last unit of its
construction expansion program begun several years ago.
Upon completion of this work, it is hoped that the Company will benefit through progressively increased use of
these modern and large facilities. Early in 1940 the voters
of the city of Springfield rejected the purchase of the

company by the city by approximately two to one. The Supreme Court of the state of Missouri by a unanimous decision stated that the company had a perpetual franchise under which the city has the privilege of purchasing the property at five-year intervals. In such an event, it is expected that a fair price would be realized."

Finally, that same report cited the refunding of Kankakee Water Company's outstanding bonds, reducing the interest rate from 6% to 4½%, and raising additional capital to pay off short-term debt and finance future improvements.

A few months later, in August 1940, a special meeting was called to address a most fortunate windfall. Beaver Falls Municipal Authority, recently formed at the urging of a municipal bond salesman, had made an offer to purchase from Beaver Valley Water Company all of its assets for $4,300,000 in cash. That offer, which would result in an after-tax gain of $596,302, would provide the Company sufficient funds after payment of Beaver Falls outstanding debt to retire all of the parent company's 6% first-mortgage bonds, all of its 5½% debentures, all of the scrip outstanding on those debentures, and all of its first preferred capital stock which, by virtue of the dividends in arrears at 7% and a call premium of $5 per share, would net those preferred shareholders $164.77 per share.

The offer was accepted, and all those burdensome securities were retired before year-end. The September 1, 1940, edition of the *Portland Sunday Telegram* included a story headlined "Maine Financial Comment: How a stock in a Portland company rose from $6 to $166.77 a share this summer, and it's not a fairy story." (The $166.77 is a $2 typo error.) A portion of the text of the article is reproduced on the facing page.

Maine Financial Comment

How A Stock In A Portland Company Rose From $6 To $166.77 A Share This Summer, And It's Not A Fairy Story

By Harold J. Boyle
Financial Editor

Every so often a financial development with a fairy story tinge happens in Maine. The latest, and probably the most unusual in many years has come about dramatically with the almost matter-of-fact announcement that the Maine-incorporated Consumers Water Company, which controls and operates water companies in several parts of the Country, has sold one of its companies—Beaver Valley Water in Beaver Valley, Penn.—to the municipality in which the water works is located. That city has decided to operate the property as a public enterprise, just like Portland owns its own water system.

Profit

Financial developments of that kind happen several times a year, but this one is different. Through the sale of the Beaver Valley company to the municipality, Consumers Water Company, which is directed by the West interests of Portland, will receive back its original investment in the Pennsylvania water property, plus a fair profit. And it will use the funds to retire $850,000 in bonds outstanding on Consumers Water Company, plus the 4,620 shares of preferred stock ahead of the holding company's common stock. And that preferred stock, which changed hands a few months ago as low as $6 a share, will be paid off—and hold your hat—at $164.77 a share, which represents the par value of $100 a share, $5 more for its call price of 105, and all unpaid dividends since the company was forced to suspend quarterly payments of $1.75 a share back in 1932. Yes, the price is $164.77 a share for a stock that sold at $6 this Summer.

Bondholders of Consumers Water, most of whom are Maine residents (and so are the preferred stockholders) also fare handsomely in this transaction. During the depression, these bonds, together with all holding company issues, declined sharply in market value. At one time, the 5½ per cent issue sold around 20 cents on the dollar. Even this year the same bonds could be purchased for 70 cents on the dollar. The other loan issue on the company, the 6s due in 1946, enjoyed a better market, selling in the 90s the past two years. But in both cases, owners will receive $1,000 a bond, plus a small premium representing the call price in advance of actual maturity. Holders of the 5½ per cent bonds also will receive cash for part of their bond interest, which was paid to them in the form of scrip (a receipt for future cash) in recent years.

Those who bought that preferred stock anywhere from $2 to $6 a share (and they are only a minority) will reap the kind of profit that comes along very few times in a generation. The Midas touch is still a fairy story.

From a Sept. 1, 1940, Portland Sunday Telegram article

Thus the Company ended the Depression with seven subsidiaries in seven states: Springfield in Missouri, Kankakee in Illinois, Shenango Valley in Pennsylvania and Ohio,[2] Plattsmouth in Nebraska, Hudson in New Hampshire, plus Freeport and Winterport in Maine. As it was in 1929, Consumers was still the only multi-state and exclusively water utility holding company in the country. General Water Works was reportedly organized during WWII. American Water Works was still a part of a diversified utility holding company, American Water Works and Electric, and Charles Mott, whose holdings eventually became Continental Water Company, was just starting to build his portfolio of water utilities. The Depression-era statute, the Public Utility Holding Company Act, eventually forced American to split in half in 1947. That statute also forced the breakup of Federal Water Service Corporation which owned electric, water and gas utilities in twelve states. You'll read more about Federal later in this book.

Interestingly enough, it was not the war that rescued Consumers from the ravages of the Depression but rather the sale of Roanoke and Beaver Valley to their respective municipalities.

---

[2] Shenango's system crosses the Pennsylvania-Ohio line, and the portion in Ohio is a subsidiary of Shenango, **Masury Water Company**.

CHAPTER FOUR

The War Years

World War II was an interesting period for Consumers Water Company. Water was not generally thought of as a vital commodity for winning a war but, in fact, it was an essential industry. Nevertheless, both materials and labor were hard to come by as the war progressed. Iron for pipe and brass for valves and fittings were rigidly controlled by the War Production Board, and allotments to the water utility industry were carefully screened. Consumers' four biggest utilities, Springfield, Plattsmouth, Kankakee and Shenango, were all located in World War II boom towns. Eight miles outside Plattsmouth, too distant to become a customer, there was a new bomber plant that, by the time the war ended, had built 1,585 B-26's and 531 B-29's. In Springfield, there was a new Army hospital and rapid growth of several small industries. A plan to supply water to an Illinois state hospital plus expanding industries in Kankakee and Bradley greatly increased the pumpage at Kankakee. And at Shenango Valley, as you might well expect, Sharon Steel swung into full production, three shifts a day, seven days a week. Adding to Shenango's demands was the large Westinghouse plant, not far from Sharon Steel, which, among other items, was manufacturing torpedoes for the Navy. All those industries required labor and, thus, a modest amount of new housing was also added to the systems.

All of Consumers' systems did meet the increased demands of the war. At Plattsmouth, the existing plant capacity was sufficient to serve the new housing for the bomber plant employees. The major expansion at Springfield that was commenced in 1937 and tripled the capacity of the treatment plant was completed in 1940. In that same year, major improvements at Sharon were started. They included a complete new steam plant, a new river intake, a new clearwell, expanded pumping capacity and new housing for both the steam plant and the treatment plant. That work was essentially completed by mid-1942. In July 1941, Kankakee executed a contract with the state of Illinois to furnish water for the State Hospital at Manteno some ten miles north of Kankakee. That precipitated the construction of both a new transmission main through Kankakee to Bradley and major improvements to the treatment plant, including a new sedimentation basin and two new filters. (The state built the line from Bradley to Manteno.) When Pearl Harbor was bombed, the work at Kankakee was just beginning, but it was completed in mid-1942. All the above construction, just in time for the peak war effort, was sufficient to carry the Consumers systems through the war, with the exception of a new seven million gallon per day pump for Shenango Valley in 1944. (War Production Board authority required.) Of course, main extensions continued through the war when and where required.

The increased pumpage presented a new problem at several of the systems. In spite of the additional capital to be supported, the increased revenue led to increased profits. At more than one system, management focused on ways to avoid a mandated rate decrease and/or the wartime excess profits tax. The solution was a liberal policy of expensing vs. capitalizing of charges and increased allowances for depreciation.

The office in Portland was also busy with World War II demands. Herman Burgi, the Company's Chief Engineer, was especially busy. Mr. Burgi was an electrical engineer who had worked for Cumberland County Power and Light until Vernon West had persuaded him to work for both Consumers and George F. West & Son. Herman quickly learned the electrical requirements of the water utility industry, and it wasn't long before he was pioneering innovative systems to increase efficiency and reduce manpower. One source reports that while Vernon West was extremely high on Herman Burgi's skills, Vernon did resist a wholesale conversion to electric pumping as witnessed by new or expanded steam plants at Springfield and Sharon.

Besides overseeing the major plant improvements in the Consumers system, Herman Burgi was also busy with work closer to home carried out by George F. West & Son. Casco Bay was the primary anchorage for the North Atlantic Convoy Fleet. To protect that fleet, thousands of troops were stationed on the major islands surrounding the anchorage. Those troops manned extensive coast artillery batteries and the submarine nets that were strung across the navigable passages between the islands. The troops required housing and other means of subsistence, including both power and water. Electricity, water and gas were supplied by Casco Bay Light and Power Company, formerly the Peaks Island Corporation. The West family had a financial interest in Casco Bay Power, and George F. West & Son enjoyed a contract for its operation. As the troop build-up progressed on the islands, the electric and water facilities were badly over-taxed, and major improvements and expansions were necessary. The power came from diesel generators, and the water from island wells. A. Vinton Lewis, an independent contractor who did much of the work for Casco Bay during the war, reported to this writer that there were many crises during that period that had to be met, frequently in less than ideal weather conditions. He cited a few examples, including the severance of the power line in Hussey Sound between Peaks and Long Islands. Apparently a Navy ship dragged its anchor across the submerged cable. Maintaining the supply of oil for the generators was a constant problem as it was hard to come by and, when it was finally available, had to be conveyed to the islands no matter what the weather. None of this was Consumers Water Company business directly, but it added to the pressures on the Portland office during the war.

The complications of wartime conditions did not divert Consumers' management from its focus on the financial success of the business. With few exceptions, rates were frozen during the war but, fortunately, pumpage and revenues were strong and increased each year as the war progressed. To some extent the increased revenues were offset by higher taxes and the carrying costs of increased debt to support the major plant expansions. One negative factor that impacted Consumers as the Depression ended was the elimination of the lucrative management contracts for both operations and capital improvements. One by one, the state public utility commissions focused on those contracts and demanded that they be terminated to prevent the parent company recovering from the subsidiaries anything but its actual costs.

On the positive side, the Company continued to focus on opportunities to minimize costs of both parent company and subsidiary debt and preferred stock. In 1945 before the war ended, Springfield refinanced almost $3.5 million of 4% first-mortgage bonds with a like amount of 3% bonds, and almost $200,000 of 11% preferred stock with 5% preferred stock. Kankakee refunded $1,000,000 of 4¼% bonds with a like amount of 3% bonds, while Shenango Valley called $485,000 of 6% preferred stock and issued a like amount of 5% preferred stock.

During the war, management also attended to its 50% interest in the Dartmouth Company[3] which was solidified by the expiration of the original buy-back options. Dartmouth still had several secured and unsecured debts outstanding that were significantly discounted since little or no interest had been paid on them since the early '30's. One by one, Consumers proceeded to purchase from banks and individuals Dartmouth's bonds and notes at steep discounts. The Company also focused on the fact that Frank Rumery owned 3,000 shares of Dartmouth preferred stock, 100% of that issue. In order to relieve Dartmouth of the requirement to pay off all of the debt issues accumulated by Consumers and place Consumers in a true 50% ownership position, in April 1945, the Company executed another agreement with Frank Rumery whereby Consumers would forgive some of the short-term indebtedness it had acquired in exchange for 1,500 of the preferred shares owned by Frank Rumery. The contract also specified

[3] The Dartmouth Real Estate Company did not change its name to the Dartmouth Company until 1982; in the interest of brevity, the shorter name is used in this book.

certain salaries and benefits for Frank Rumery and his son, Earl, and included an incentive to reduce Dartmouth's first-mortgage bonds outstanding to $500,000.

The sale of Plattsmouth Water Company, anticipated at the start of the war, came to pass in 1943. The negotiations had started with the city offering $100,000 and the Company demanding $300,000. The final price was almost $217,000, which netted Consumers a gain of over $25,000. The sale was characterized in the Company's 1943 Annual Report as less than "its full and fair value," but the Company was not disappointed to lose Plattsmouth since its location was not a good fit with the rest of the system.

Also in 1943, founding Director George F. West died. At the annual meeting the next year, John McInnes, another partner at H.M. Payson Co., was elected to the board.

There was one other item that required attention of the Company officers during the war. Upon filing tax returns that included the sale of the Beaver Valley and Roanoke water systems, there arose with the federal government a disagreement as to the appropriate tax basis of those systems and, thus, the capital gains tax. The Company had paid the tax it believed to be appropriate, but the IRS was claiming an additional $471,804. Periodically during the war, revenue agents met with lawyers, accountants and officers of the Company, but by the end of the war, the matter was yet to be settled. There was a distinct possibility that the case would go to court.

Thus, when the war ended, Consumers had one less subsidiary, but its remaining plants were in sound condition and its financial posture was significantly improved. Management was anticipating a post-war boom arising from accumulated savings, pent up demand for goods of all kinds, and a need for thousands of new housing units.

CHAPTER FIVE

Post-war to the Sale of Springfield

As it was during the war, there was little growth in the decade after the war for Consumers' two small Maine utilities, Freeport and Winterport. In New Hampshire, across the river from Nashua, the Hudson system did start to grow. The three larger properties, however, continued to experience the most growth. Fortunately, both Kankakee and Shenango Valley were faced with no supply problems. Both utilities drew only a minor fraction of the river flowage adjacent to their treatment plants. Kankakee experienced the most dramatic growth. Following the 1940 census, the government revealed that the geographically weighted population center of the forty-eight states had moved west to a point within a few miles of Kankakee, Illinois. Thus, several major national companies focused on Kankakee as an ideal spot to locate a new plant.

Armstrong Cork actually broke ground well before the
end of the war. Close on its heels with new plants were: A.
O. Smith Corporation, Borden Milk Company, and General Mills Corporation. A little later, Armour built a meat
packing plant. In addition, Kankakee State Hospital, Romy
Hammes, David Bradley Manufacturing Company and
Kohler Manufacturing Company made extensive improvements and plant additions. All that new business, of course,
required extensive new labor which, in response to the
opportunities, was migrating south to Kankakee from
Chicago. And, to serve the growing populace, both Sears
Roebuck and Montgomery Ward proceeded with new and
larger outlets while Pepsi Cola installed a new bottling
plant. This, in turn, forced Kankakee Water Company to
further expand its plant capacity and install numerous
water main extensions and reinforcements.

Fortunately, new capital for all this work was relatively
inexpensive. Those circumstances also allowed the subsidiaries to further reduce the costs of their senior capital.
In 1947 Springfield sold an additional $500,000 of 3%
bonds while Freeport Water Company refinanced its small
4% mortgage and bank borrowings with a new 3% mortgage note. Dartmouth called in over $500,000 of $4\frac{1}{2}\%$
bonds and issued $525,000 of $3\frac{1}{2}\%$ first-mortgage bonds.

Shenango Valley Water Company successfully refinanced but only after a struggle with the Pennsylvania Public Utilities Commission that lasted over five years. The
problem came to a head in 1942 when the Pennsylvania
PUC noticed that after the successful reorganization and
refinancing following Consumers' purchase of the company in 1926, Consumers had only $10,000 invested in that
multi-million dollar company. The PUC could not abide
Consumers earning the normal profit of a multi-million

dollar utility with only $10,000 invested. Thus, it stonewalled any further debt financing by Shenango and, instead, demanded that Consumers invest additional money in Shenango Valley's capital stock account. This turned out to be a significant drain on the parent company's available cash. By 1947, following numerous infusions of paid-in capital, Shenango's equity account had climbed to $300,000. At that point, the Pennsylvania PUC decided to mandate a new system of accounts which required a complete inventory of the entire water utility plant and a recreation of its original cost. This was a monumental task that consumed much time and significant outside help. For another year or two, the dispute continued over the proper original cost figures, the proper amount of depreciation that had been accrued, and the continuing requirement of the parent company to infuse additional equity.

To further complicate the situation, wages and the cost of material in that post-war period increased annually, and the utility was in desperate need of increased rates merely to break even. But the PUC would not allow a rate increase until disputed items were settled. Shenango's General Manager during that period was a first-class engineer, J. Porter Hennings, who had been hired in Portland and shortly thereafter shipped out to that western Pennsylvania steel mill town. Porter was a native of Maine, educated at Orono, and well equipped to handle the post-war growth and the day-to-day operations of the utility. But he was not comfortable playing the game of chicken mandated from the Portland office insofar as capital improvements and creditors were concerned. It is reported that near the end of the scenario, Porter would rarely be seen on the streets of Sharon because of his fear of running into company creditors or business leaders pushing for more rapid expansion of the utility. Finally, in 1950, Porter resigned when he learned of an opportunity to return to Portland and become Chief Engineer of the Portland Water District.[4]

This was not the first valuable employee the Company lost in the post-war era. A year earlier, in 1949, Herman Burgi also resigned to join the Portland Water District. It is reported that Herman tired of the grueling traveling schedule that was required to be effective in his job. Bear in mind that in those days, travel was primarily by train rather than airplane, and, thus, to visit two or three of the larger subsidiaries, a five-day trip was mandatory. It appeared that Herman Burgi was destined for bigger things since only a year after joining Portland Water District, he became General Manager, a position he held for the next fourteen years. It is quite likely that Herman Burgi had a hand in Porter Hennings' decision to join the District as well.

On the other hand, the Company had gained in the post-war era two extremely valuable employees, either one of whom had the potential to become President of the Company. The first was John W. L. White, hired in 1946. John came to the Company with an MIT degree in Business and Engineering Administration, ideal training for the water utility industry. He spent his entire career in the Portland office and, after the departure of Herman Burgi and the passage of the Maine Professional Engineer's Exam, was appointed Company Engineer. A couple of years after John was hired, a new salary schedule was approved by the board that set John's compensation at $400 per month. That was significant since the same schedule set Fletcher Means' salary at $300 per month. At that time John White, relatively new to the Company, was classified as Engineer in

---

[4] The Portland Water District is the same utility as the Portland Water Company which Henry M. Payson helped survive in the 1870's. Porter completed his career at PWD, serving as its General Manager from 1975 to 1978.

John J. Russell, left, a highly valued officer and director, and William B. Skelton, right, a key founding director.

Training, whereas Fletcher had almost twenty years of service and was both an officer and a director of the Company. It appeared that Vernon West was suppressing the salary of his younger cousin.

The second valued employee, John Russell, joined the Company in 1950, immediately after graduating from Bowdoin College with a Liberal Arts degree. That background quickly proved to be no handicap. It wasn't long before he could hold his own with engineers, accountants and lawyers. Many from each of those specialities thought John had had formal training in their field. John was soon sent to Kankakee as Assistant Manager under General Manager Lynn Minor. In late 1956, following the death of Springfield's General Manager, Jasper W. Everett, John was transferred to Springfield to oversee that operation while the final touches were applied to the Fellows Lake Dam and the company was preparing for the city take-over.

In addition to the Shenango Valley problem, another

festering situation further aggravated Consumers' cash flow. In 1947, the $472,000 tax dispute over the sale of Roanoke Water Works Company and Beaver Valley Water Company was finally concluded. Shortly after the war, the Company reluctantly agreed to a $120,000 settlement on the Roanoke dispute, but the Beaver Valley situation endured longer. In the end, the Company had no choice but to agree to an additional tax of $250,000 plus back interest, making the total for Beaver Valley $321,306. The Company simply could not afford to litigate the matter further, especially with the accumulating interest. But neither did it have the cash to pay the bill. (It had paid the additional Roanoke tax out of cash flow.)

The best alternative, and certainly not an attractive one, was for the Parent to sell to an insurance company $300,000 of $3\frac{3}{4}\%$, 10-year, collateral trust bonds. The collateral terms mandated that the Company deposit with the Trustee for the duration of the issue all of the Company's common stock in Shenango Valley Water Company, Springfield City Water Company, and Kankakee Water Company plus $287,000 of General Mortgage and Promissory Notes of the Dartmouth Company that Consumers held in its treasury. Once again, the parent company was both leveraged and tied up in knots.

Meanwhile, advantageous refinancing continued. In spite of its dispute with the Pennsylvania PUC, the Commission allowed Shenango to refinance existing issues. The last of its 6% Preferred Stock was converted into 5% Preferred Stock, $1.5 million of 4% First Mortgage Bonds were called and, along with some bank notes, refinanced with $1.7 million of $2\frac{7}{8}\%$ First Mortgage Bonds. Such a coupon rate reflected what had to be a period of the cheapest money of the Twentieth Century. The cost of long-term

debt money is normally made up of three elements, namely:
  (1) the market demand for interest, normally about 3%,
  (2) an allowance for risk, which for utility bonds is normally at least 1% over long-term treasuries,
  (3) and an allowance for anticipated inflation.

Now look at the circumstances for Shenango's 1947 bond issue. With zero inflation, Shenango's bond rates would normally be 3% for interest plus 1% for risk. But instead of being zero, inflation for '45, '46, and '47 was 2.3%, 8.3% and 14.4% respectively. For long-term bonds in 1947, it certainly appeared that inflation would be a significant factor. A normal inflation add-on to the 3% plus 1% would have been 5% to 8%, making the total rate 9%–12%. The only rationale this author can imagine for a $2\frac{7}{8}\%$ interest rate was that supply and demand factors were totally negating the normal elements of money costs.

During this period, the possibility of Consumers losing one, or all three, of its large utilities was real. At Springfield, a take-over of the water company had been rejected by the voters in 1940, but that was due in a large degree to the fact that the city was preoccupied with taking over both the electric company serving the city and the local gas company. It was only a matter of time before the water utility would rise to the top of the list. In July 1949, a Philadelphia bond house convinced the Mayor of Sharon that that city should take over Shenango Valley Water Company. The Company's official response to the Mayor was that if the majority of the voters and special interest groups, such as organized labor and local businesses, endorsed the take-over, and a fair price could be reached, the Company would be willing to sell.

Dartmouth's Ricker Park Garden Apartments, also designed by John P. Thomas

Similarly, in 1950 the city of Kankakee approached the Company for the take-over of that utility. In October of that year, Consumers actually entered into an agreement with McDougal and Company, another bond house, which was appointed by the city to represent its interests. The agreement was lengthy and outlined how the property would be appraised and, if that could be agreed upon, how a purchase would be carried out. Eventually, even though the Payson interests were reportedly receptive to a liquidation of the Company, both the Shenango and Kankakee efforts ran out of steam.

For most, if not all, of Consumers' subsidiaries, there had been no rate increase from the 1929 crash through the end of the war. Post-war inflation and plant expansion, however, mandated rate increases if the subsidiary companies were to remain solvent. Thus, commencing in 1948, the Company initiated an aggressive program seeking increases in rates in all of its subsidiaries. This was basically unfamiliar territory, not just for the Company, but also for several of the public utility commissions involved. Higher rates, therefore, came neither easily nor quickly.

Until the new rates came into effect, cash flow was a major problem of the Company. In addition to the cash required for the growth of the three large subsidiaries, the new $300,000 collateral trust bond issue called for a $30,000 annual sinking fund payment. Fortunately, the Dartmouth Company was doing quite well, and for several years provided all the cash necessary for the sinking fund. Dartmouth's favorable cash flow was coming from the A&P Warehouse on Kennebec Street, the 509 Forest Avenue office building, most of which was leased to Associated Hospital Service of Maine (predecessor to Maine Blue Cross/Blue Shield), several automobile dealerships on Forest Avenue, and the Ricker Park Garden Apartments.

In May 1951, a major change in management occurred. At the organizational board meeting for the year, President West, as was customary, opened the meeting. Then, before he could proceed further, some unusual events occurred. Immediately after the opening, the minutes read, "On motion duly made and seconded, it was unanimously

VOTED: To elect William B. Skelton Chairman of the meeting."

Mr. Skelton, almost eighty, had been re-elected to the board at the annual shareholders meeting earlier that year. Given the event that was about to occur, it is easy to speculate that the Paysons had contacted Bill and urged him to rejoin the board to assist them in an unpleasant task. By then he had stepped down as President of Central Maine Power and was winding down the affairs of NEPSCO, of which he was still President. Thus, he apparently felt that he again had time to devote to Consumers' board.

Then, following some reports on the operating companies by Vernon West and Fletcher Means, "Director Harold C. Payson reported that President Vernon F. West had indicated a desire to be relieved of some of his duties. It was his recommendation that President West be named Chairman of the Board of Directors...." It was further recommended "that Director Payson (Harold) be elected President of the Company without salary, (and) that Fletcher W. Means be elected Vice President and General Manager to assume the duties relinquished by Mr. West, etc." The votes that followed put those recommendations into effect.

It appears that Vernon West's relationship with the board had become strained. A year earlier for the board meeting preceding the annual organizational board meeting, the minutes read, "The President further stated that if the amount owed by him to Consumers Water Company was not liquidated prior to or on July 31, 1950, he would not be a candidate for re-election as President of the Company." The notes had been paid off in full on July 24, 1950 and he was, therefore, re-elected. A year and a half before that, approximately $46,500 of notes owed to the Company by George F. West & Son became due (not for the first time) and were renewed by a demand note from Vernon West, making his total indebtedness to the Company approximately $58,500. At that time the Company allowed him a sweetheart interest rate of 2%.

From accounts passed down over the years, it is also known that Vernon West's interests had, in fact, digressed from the Company and that he was spending more and more time at his ranch in Arizona. There are also stories of how Vernon's expense accounts and cash advances for same were scantily documented and quite liberal. His frequent trips to his ranch in Arizona invariably involved calls at one or more of the Company's western subsidiaries and, thus, were treated as business trips. Also noteworthy is the fact that Vernon West was absent from the regular board meeting preceding the fateful May 25, 1951, board meeting, to the best of this writer's research, the first board meeting he missed in his twenty-five years of service.

The above facts, however, give an unfair impression. Vernon West was clearly the driving force for the creation of a very successful company. He was a brilliant businessman, and the corporate records are replete with reports and recommendations from Vernon to the board that clearly reveal an outstanding grasp of both the financial and engineering nuances of the water utility industry. They further reveal a solid appreciation of local politics, appropriate relations with public utility commissions, and a sensitivity to customer needs. While a few of the major diversified utility companies of his time accumulated larger portfolios that included water utilities, Vernon West was clearly the leading water utility entrepreneur in the country and most successful at it. As already stated, his term of office was by far the longest in the history of the Company, and he can surely be forgiven for a divergence of interest as he approached retirement.

Another aspect to recognize is that while he created and preserved a tremendous amount of wealth for the Company shareholders, his salary from Consumers was modest, even for the standards of his time. There were no senior officer perks such as stock options and bonuses, and during his entire reign the shares he owned received only two modest cash dividends in the early '30's. He benefited from no company life or health insurance policies nor any formal retirement plan. He did, however, receive a generous salary as Chairman of the board after his retirement.

Vernon was well known for his lifestyle. He lived in a grand house on Falmouth Foreside, owned a large yacht that he enjoyed as Commodore of at the Portland Yacht Club, and drove around in fancy cars that were probably never furnished by the Company. One of his still living relatives reports that his major problem was that he could not resist living beyond his means.

Harold C. Payson, a partner at H.M. Payson Co. and Consumers' second president.

The new organization was, of course, unusual. Harold Payson, one of the founding directors, was still a full-time partner at H.M. Payson Co. After over twenty years with the Company, Fletcher Means was ready to be President. It is reported that the reason for the odd set-up was to shield Fletcher from his domineering cousin and, thus, give Fletcher a chance to run the Company in his own way. Under the circumstances, it was probably the optimum solution.

The salary adjustment votes that follow the change in officers are also fascinating. They were dictated by the Korean War anti-inflation statute, the Wage Stabilization Act, which placed limitations on salary and wage increases. As Chairman, Vernon West's salary was reduced by the first series of votes from $570 per month to $300 per month while Fletcher's was increased from $300 to $520 per month. The next vote granted Fletcher a further increase of $55 per month and John White an increase of $90 per month. There was then a further vote that increased the officers' salaries even more, including Vernon West's from $300 to $400 per month, Fletcher Means' from $575 to $600 per month, and John White's from $490 to $500 per month. The second and third salary adjustment votes were both conditioned on approval by the Wage Stabilization Board. (Besides serving as Chairman, Vernon's new duties called for significant hours of consultation and missionary service in the Company's endeavors for harmonious community relations and increased rates.)

Further documentation of Fletcher Means' true status in the Company is that the Annual Report to Consumers' stockholders for 1950 was submitted not by Harold Payson, President, but rather by Fletcher Means, General Manager.[5]

That report, incidentally, makes it clear why Consumers had not yet resumed, after a twenty-four-year moratorium, a cash dividend on its common stock. The Company was consistently profitable, but the general policy of the state regulatory commissions (and sound financing) was to require at least 35% of capital expenditures to be financed by increased equity capital. Springfield, Kankakee and Shenango Valley were still experiencing vigorous growth, and, thus, every dollar that could be accumulated had to meet that need. Without the Dartmouth Real Estate Company, Consumers would have had a real problem since there was not yet an established public market for raising additional equity through a common stock offering.

In light of the above-cited explanation, the shareholders must have been surprised to learn later that year that the Company had voted Dividend #3, 10 cents per share, payable September 1, 1951. That was certainly a wonderful way for the new regime to start out. Another positive note was that in October of that year the contract enabling the city of Kankakee to purchase the water utility was allowed

---

[5] The report was issued after the May 1951 board meeting.

to expire following the city council's refusal to adopt an ordinance of purchase. At about the same time, the Wage Stabilization Board approved the requested salary increases, but a similar board rejected a request by the Dartmouth Company to increase the rents of its garden apartments.

The repeated cycles of large capital expenditures followed by new subsidiary bond financings and further rate increases continued through the 1950's.

The first significant move made by Fletcher occurred in November 1952. He called for a timekeeping system that would enable the Company to convincingly document what the people in the Portland office were doing and thereby justify reimbursement for same by the subsidiary companies. Processing subsidiary rate cases had become an everyday affair, and increasingly the state public utility commissions were balking at allowing parent company charges supported only by vague statements that the Portland people were performing tasks that were appropriate and necessary for the subsidiary companies to provide service. This change brought to a head the relationship between Consumers Water Company and George F. West & Son. Documentation of the new procedures revealed that George F. West & Son was performing management and consulting services for Biddeford & Saco Water Company, Casco Bay Light and Power Company, Leadville (Colorado) Water Company, Newport (Maine) Water Company and itself, George F. West & Son. Basically, Consumers was operating the utilities it owned, and, over the years, George F. West & Son had evolved from a water utility construction company to an unregulated utility management company. Further, Vernon West, Fletcher Means, and founding director and officer, James Coburn, were not working full time for Consumers since they also worked part time for George F. West & Son. All along they had been on the payrolls of both companies. That revealed the reason for the relatively modest salaries from Consumers previously cited for Vernon West and Fletcher Means.

The new system abolished the George F. West & Son payroll and placed everybody 100% on Consumers' payroll. With Vernon West virtually retired, the move inevitably led to the winding down of George F. West & Son. The final step of the new procedure was for Consumers to submit for PUC approval detailed contracts with each of its subsidiaries whereby the parent company would provide a multitude of services at cost. The Company also entered into similar contracts with the previous clients of George F. West & Son providing similar services but at a rate of fully allocated costs plus 10%. Such arrangements basically put George F. West & Son out of business, but there was one other new contract, namely the one between Consumers and Vernon West, whereby Consumers would attend to several of Vernon's interests at cost plus 10%. The wisdom of the overall change is documented by the fact that the system established, and the contracts drawn up, remained essentially unchanged for the balance of the life of Consumers Water Company.

By far the knottiest operating problem of the post-war era was water supply at Springfield. Solution of the problem was not merely a matter of raising and spending large sums of money but, more important, determining where to spend it. When the West family was first involved in the early 1900's, Springfield was a small town, and its water utility was supplied by wells. Around 1920, Vernon West hired Philip Burgess of Burgess & Niple (subsequently a founding director of Consumers) to make a study to determine how the utility might obtain additional supplies of water. At that time, the local consensus was that the nearby James River was the logical choice for a storage reservoir and raw water transmission main. Phil Burgess, however, concluded that, for the foreseeable needs, a preferable source was the Little Sack River and, thus, in the early '20's prior to Consumers' acquisition of the utility, a reservoir was built that formed McDaniel Lake, and Springfield's water supply problem was apparently solved. With the rapid growth during World War II and the years following, however, it was soon apparent that McDaniel Lake's supply must be augmented. After acquiring Kankakee Water Company, Vernon West developed a relationship with Louis R. Howson of the Chicago firm Alvord, Burdick, and Howson, primarily for engineering work at Kankakee. When it was time to build a new plant at Springfield, Alvord, Burdick, and Howson was selected for the engineering design, and Burgess and Niple was awarded a contract to administer the construction. As previously cited, the facility was completed in 1940 and named the Fulbright Treatment Plant (*see dust jacket photo*).

Thus, in 1947, Springfield Water Company engaged both Burgess & Niple and Alvord, Burdick and Howson to independently submit studies and recommendations for supplementing the water supply. Interestingly enough, these two highly respected engineering firms came up with conflicting reports, each advocating what it felt was the most economical solution. Louis Howson recommended another reservoir on the Little Sack River, upstream from McDaniel Lake, while, this time around, Director Burgess recommended the construction of a reservoir on the James River. That threw Consumers' management into a quandary compounded by the fact that one of the professionals was a member of its own board. Also complicating the situation was the fact that Vernon West outspokenly favored the Howson solution. Because of a lack of a clear direction, the situation festered for several years.

As far as water supply was concerned, the utility was clearly on borrowed time but through 1951 enjoyed average or above average rainfall. In 1952, however, the circumstances changed as an extended drought developed. 1953 was the driest year in the history of the area, and the drought continued through 1954. With the exception of Phil Burgess and Vernon West, Consumers' board did not know which way to go. Accordingly, in June of 1953, a third reputable engineering firm, Malcolm Pirnie Engineers from New York, was hired to evaluate the Burgess and Howson reports and whatever other circumstances they deemed appropriate and advise the board which way to go. Although following a somewhat different line of logic, Malcolm Pirnie agreed with the Howson recommendation. Feelings were obviously running high, especially between Phil Burgess and Vernon West. In fact, in a letter of eleven typewritten pages to the Consumers board dated April 23, 1954, Phil Burgess cites a quote from the Pirnie engagement letter written and signed by Vernon West, namely, "As a result of this study, we hope a plan of procedure can be recommended to us that will fit into our present plan of development." Phil Burgess then states, "In view of the fact that Mr. West in 1948 had taken a position that future water supply at Springfield could best be obtained by constructing a storage reservoir on the Little Sack River above McDaniel Lake, the above quotation would seem to be a direct request that Mr. Pirnie approve this plan." Phil Burgess also cites in his letter the fact that at the hearing before the Missouri Public Service Commission seeking approval of the project, only the Howson and Pirnie reports were submitted for evidence with virtually no acknowledgment of the existence of the Burgess report. The Burgess letter goes on to admit that unsolicited on February 16, 1954, Phil Burgess wrote the Missouri Commission advising them of his study and his recommendation that the James River was a better alternative. He further states, "In writing this letter I had appreciated that I was taking an unusual action, but I also appreciated that the situation was unusual. The management of Springfield City Water Company had suppressed our formal report for several years, and I had reason to expect that it would suppress my present report if it could possibly do so." It is not surprising that the following March, prior to the completion of his current term, Phil Burgess tendered his resignation from Consumers' board of directors. The Missouri Commission did approve construction of the second Little Sack River dam that eventually formed the largest body of water in the Springfield area, Fellows Lake.

Springfield did not survive its drought unscathed. In a Letter to Shareholders dated April 28, 1954, Fletcher Means stated, "… In the latter part of January 1954, for the first time in the company's history, or since 1883, the water utility customers in Springfield were requested to conserve water." In actuality, more drastic measures were required. System pressures were reduced, and the old wells were reconditioned and pressed into service. In early 1954, the situation was getting desperate, and the company employed a cloud-seeding company from Denver in an effort to bring on some rain. The results of the cloud seeding apparently were minimal, at best, and finally, in March of that year, the company proceeded to install a temporary, emergency, above-ground, five-mile water main from the

James River along with a complete, albeit temporary, water treatment plant and clearwell to augment the supply. The entire project was completed in twenty-four days, a near miracle. Of course, it was ironic that the fastest, most economical relief, however temporary, came from the James River, a point that was not ignored in Phil Burgess' letter of April 23. Then, on July 8, 1954, the city of Springfield filed a formal complaint with the Missouri Public Service Commission alleging that in spite of constant growth, "the company has negligently failed to improve its source of water supply during the last twenty years...."

In several pages the complaint documents the inadequate action taken by the company and the emergency measures imposed upon the citizens of Springfield. Among other things, the city's complaint second-guesses the company's decision and the Commission's approval of the company's intent to construct a new reservoir on the Little Sack River rather than the James. Concurrently, the city was engaged in a new dialogue with the company concerning its take-over by the city, and it certainly appears that the formal complaint was filed to strengthen the case and gain public approval for a take-over of the company. A contract for the construction of the Fellows Lake Dam was let on October 14, 1954, with the total cost of the project estimated to be $2,600,000. By necessity, in an unprecedented and never to be repeated move, Consumers' board authorized the parent company to guarantee construction loans of its subsidiary to complete the project.

The dam construction was essentially completed in early November 1955. A dedication ceremony was held on November 11 at which city officials, company officials, contractors, and representatives from the interested banks, insurance companies and engineering firms were present.

One of the more colorful stories handed down over the years reveals that following the ceremony, a few of the visiting dignitaries decided to go duck hunting on the company's lake (McDaniel) early the next morning. They committed a fatal error, however, by talking about their plan too loudly at a local pub that evening. The next morning they were apprehended during their joyful outing for hunting without licenses and had to post bail before they could leave town.

The new impoundment which, when full, would hold seven times as much water as McDaniel Lake, was named in memory of H. F. Fellows, an original incorporator and first President of Springfield City Water Company, who had died in 1894. By the time the dam project was completed, Springfield's capitalization ratios were completely out of balance. The company had $6 million of bonds outstanding and $4 million of short-term debt (guaranteed by Consumers) which, amounting to 78% of the total capitalization, was far too high. The company needed a large infusion of new equity capital. Since a sale of the company in the not too distant future was anticipated, it was in Consumers' best interest that it at least maintain, if not increase, its percentage ownership of the common stock, namely, 75%.

Thus, in May 1956, Consumers issued to an insurance company $1 million of "sinking fund debentures" and, as Springfield sold new stock, utilized the debenture proceeds, plus additional cash, to maintain its interest in Springfield at slightly over 75%. By then, the collateral trust debentures of 1947 had been completely retired, and this time around the Company's credit was such that a collateral trust agreement was not required. Moreover, the new financing for Springfield included first-mortgage bonds to pay off the balance of Springfield's short-term indebtedness, which, in turn, released Consumers' guarantee.

In August 1956, there was another reorganization of the Company which proved to be short-lived. James Coburn resigned as a director of the Company and Fletcher Means dropped his title as General Manager of the Company. Richard N. Berry, an experienced water utility engineer, was hired to become General Manager of the Company reporting to Fletcher and also to fill the vacant board seat of

Fletcher W. Means, Consumers Water Company president from 1957 to 1966

James Coburn. The rationale was that Fletcher needed assistance in running the Company. However, within little over a year, James Coburn, who was over seventy, had elected to retire from active service with the Company, and Dick Berry had tendered his resignation.

John White was then tapped to fill the vacancies. In successive moves, he was elected Treasurer of the Company, Clerk of the Company, and Secretary to the board of directors. In addition, he was elected by the board to fill the vacant seat of Dick Berry. Moreover, following the annual shareholder meeting of 1957, Fletcher Means was elected President of the Company, thus relieving Harold Payson of that part-time, no compensation responsibility.

On February 19, 1957, after years of backing and filling

and many months of valuations and negotiations, a contract was executed for the sale of the utility plant of Springfield City Water Company to the city for a base price of $19 million. The contract was subject to approval by the citizens of Springfield, acceptable financing for the purchase, and approval by the Missouri Public Service Commission. In due course, all three conditions were met, and on December 30, 1957, in New York City, the assets were sold and the Company relinquished control of the utility. Consumers had sold only one of its six water utility subsidiaries, but in one swoop it had lost approximately 58% of its net utility plant.

CHAPTER SIX

Rebuilding the Portfolio

The sale of Springfield City Water Company was by far the most significant event in the history of Consumers Water Company. On a consolidated basis, the Company eventually booked a gain, net of taxes and expenses, of over $3.75 million. Overnight, the Company's book value per share doubled from $15.49 to $31.09.

The circumstances presented a real dilemma to the board. The potential earning power of its subsidiaries was cut in half and seriously jeopardized their ability to support the Portland office. The board was basically faced with three options, namely:

(1) sell the balance of its portfolio and close up shop,

(2) pay out the lion's share of the gain to the shareholders and keep on trucking, or

(3) retain the gain and aggressively attempt to rebuild the portfolio.

The board elected the third option. To avoid double taxation, Springfield had to be liquidated within twelve months. As it was liquidated, the proceeds were passed on to the shareholders, Consumers receiving 75%. It was determined that after paying off the debentures issued to maintain Consumers' 75% interest in the subsidiary, the best temporary use of the remaining money was in tax-free municipals. Interestingly enough, since the city of Springfield had trouble selling all of its $22 million of revenue bonds issued to buy the water utility, Consumers ended up buying $3 million of those bonds.

The sale of Springfield precipitated another management change for the Company. After the closing, John Russell returned to Portland, was elected a Vice President, and became an assistant to President Means. John had had an interesting year at Springfield. Not long after he arrived, it was noticed that the new reservoir was not filling as fast as anticipated, and it was soon discovered that water was leaking through the limestone under and next to the dam. That is ironic because, in association with the engineering studies for the location of a new reservoir, a detailed geologic study predicted that in the vicinity of the proposed Little Sack Dam, there would likely be significant ground seepage. The conclusion of that geologic study was one of the many reasons Phil Burgess felt so strongly that a James River location would be preferable. John Russell's widow, Hannah Russell, reports that John lost many a night's sleep worrying about and trying to deal with the leaks. The problem was finally solved by injecting thousands of cubic yards of cement grout, the cost of which was originally estimated to be less than $100,000 but eventually cost $165,000.

There is one other noteworthy item in connection with the sale of Springfield. Since that subsidiary was acquired

A few of the many leaks through the porous limestone adjacent to the spillway of the brand-new dam for Fellows Lake. Before the area was sealed with 10,620 bags of cement grout, the dam was leaking approximately 1 million gallons per day.

in 1930, Vernon West had been its President. After Vernon had retired in 1951 and become a consultant, he continued to be the Company's front man insofar as the negotiations for the sale to the city were concerned. Not long after the sales contract was executed in 1957, the Company's long-term attorney in Springfield wrote Consumers' board recommending that Vernon West be awarded a bonus for his key role in negotiating the final sales price. Among other things, he noted that on more than one occasion he (the attorney) and Louis Howson, also participating in the negotiations, urged Vernon to make some concessions (primarily price) in order to keep the negotiations on track. Vernon, and Vernon alone, refused to compromise and eventually, thanks to his efforts, a full fair value contract was executed, thereby preserving well over a million dollars of additional final proceeds. While cutting back the recommended award, the board did eventually vote a special bonus of $50,000, not unreasonable given the money saved, but certainly a tidy sum in those days.

While Consumers was about to launch an aggressive acquisition program, another party became interested in acquiring Consumers. Less than two months after Phil Burgess resigned from the board in 1955, Albert L. Sylvester and J. Albert M. Thomas were elected to the board by the shareholders. Messrs. Sylvester and Thomas were business associates and had the reputation of being security speculators. During the '50's, it was no secret that the city of Springfield was on a course to acquire its water utility, and, smelling a big gain in the future, the two speculators gradually accumulated Consumers stock. Mr. Sylvester alone owned or controlled about 22% of the shares outstanding, much of which came from Vernon West who was selling stock to support his lifestyle. It was, therefore, consistent with Consumers' general policy of granting major shareholders a board seat, to place them in nomination for the 1955 shareholder meeting. Interestingly enough, Al Sylvester may well have accelerated Fletcher Means' promotion to President. Shortly before that event, he wrote several letters to Harold Payson criticizing how the Company was being run and suggesting, among other things, that it was time for Fletcher to be elected President.

However, once the Springfield sale was consummated, Messrs. Sylvester and Thomas went looking for greener pastures. They soon found an eager buyer for their stock, namely, Howard Butcher III who, during and following World War II, had put together another multi-state water utility holding company, General Water Works. Howard Butcher was a well-known financier associated with the firm Butcher and Sherrerd of Philadelphia. Thus, in January

1958, Messrs. Sylvester and Thomas sold their stock to Howard Butcher and/or General Water Works and promptly resigned from Consumers' board of directors.

Within a week, both Fletcher Means and Harold Payson received a letter from Howard Butcher, under General Water Works' letterhead, announcing that "we" had bought some Consumers shares, with a copy of the letter to his business associate, W. Frederick Spence. The letter was polite and friendly but, in less than a month, Consumers' shareholders began receiving letters from at least two brokerage firms encouraging them to sell their stock. Consumers' board was confident that among the Paysons and Wests and other "friends," they could control over 50% of the stock. But, nevertheless, on April 1, the Company mailed a letter to all shareholders advising them that it appeared General Water Works was attempting to gain control of the Company. The letter went on to articulate the long-term plans of the Company following the sale of Springfield, and the shareholders were encouraged to retain their stock. Less than a month later, the announcement of the upcoming annual meeting was mailed to the shareholders, and both Howard Butcher III and W. Frederick Spence were included on the slate of nominees. Each nominee, however, was identified as either "representing management interests" or "representing General Water Works Corporation interests." On April 30, the entire slate was approved and, thus, Howard Butcher and Frederick Spence came on the board. John Russell was also elected a director for the first time.

It wasn't long, however, before the old guard directors concluded that they would have to get rid of the skunks at their lawn party. Not only were they attempting to pull off a hostile take-over, but also their presence gave them inside

information on Consumers' potential acquisitions. General
Water Works itself was every bit as anxious to acquire the
same properties. Among other things, General Water
Works already had properties in at least two of the states
where Consumers was operating, namely, Maine and Pennsylvania. Eventually the old guard concluded that a direct
approach was the best solution, and Fletcher Means was
assigned the task. Fletcher met with Howard Butcher and
convinced him that he could never acquire 50% of Consumers stock. Mr. Butcher ultimately agreed and, to make
things easy for General Water Works, Consumers arranged
to purchase their shares. Fortunately, the proceeds from
the Springfield sale were available for the task. Thus, Consumers purchased for its treasury 74,367 shares, reducing
the shares outstanding by one-third. Since the price paid
was a modest premium over book value, it is assumed that
Howard Butcher et al. made a handsome profit from the
brief episode. After selling the shares, Messrs. Butcher and
Spence, of course, resigned from the board.

George S. Payson, another partner at H.M. Payson Co.,
was elected to fill one of the seats. A year later, in 1960,
Phillips M. Payson resigned and his son, Eliot B. Payson,
was elected to fill his seat. In January 1963, Harold C.
Payson died, and a month later, David R. Hastings, II, an
attorney from Fryeburg, Maine, was elected to the board to
represent his family's interests. At the annual meeting that
year, Vernon F. West stepped down and another large stockholder, Benjamin R. Alexander, an insurance executive
from the Boston area, was elected to fill his seat.

The first utility targeted by Consumers was **Camden
and Rockland Water Company** in Maine. It so happened
that General Water Works was already attempting to gain
control of Camden and Rockland (C&R). C&R had run

Mirror Lake, the primary source for Camden and Rockland Water Company. In the 1980's, Mirror Lake qualified for an exemption from the EPA mandate to filter surface water.

into hard times and was on the verge of defaulting on its maturing bonds. General Water Works' approach to the situation was to purchase the bonds from the insurance company that held them and, as soon as C&R defaulted, General Water Works would be in a position to take over the company at a distressed price. When Consumers discovered what was going on, Fletcher successfully negotiated with both the directors of C&R and its banks to go along with Consumers' plan. The banks agreed to advance C&R the funds required to pay off the bonds, the C&R directors agreed to support Consumers' tender for the C&R stock, and Consumers agreed to support C&R as it worked out its financial problems. In early 1959, Consumers purchased just over 90% of C&R's common stock.

Consumers' next acquisition was not until 1962, and it was a small one. The Company acquired all of the common shares of **Newport** (Maine) **Water Company** by an exchange of stock. Consumers/George F. West & Son had been operating Newport since before the founding of the Company in 1926. Coincidentally, Herman Burgi represented the interests of the Newport shareholders.

Less than a year later, the Company acquired another small Maine utility, **Wilton Water Company**, which had been owned by the Bass family and its company in Wilton, Bass Shoes. That purchase, too, was accomplished by an exchange of stock.

The next year, 1964, the Company's acquisition program picked up more momentum. Two more Maine subsidiaries were added, **Wiscasset Water Company** and **Damariscotta-Newcastle Water Company**. In addition, for the first time a New Jersey company was acquired, **Blackwood Water Company**, not far from the city of Camden.

The year 1965 concluded the spurt of activity with the acquisition of **Hamilton Square Water Company** near Trenton, New Jersey, and **Wanakah Water Company**, in yet another new state, just outside of Buffalo, New York. Both those companies were acquired for stock, Wanakah with preferred and Hamilton Square with common. The majority shareholder of Hamilton Square, Albert Hauptfuhrer, was quickly elected to the board.

A year earlier there had been another board change. At the age of 92, William B. Skelton died. Although he had been off the board from 1932 to 1951, he was the last of the original seven entrepreneurs to leave the Company for good. At the 1964 annual meeting, his son, William L. Skelton, was elected to represent their family interests. William L. was on the board for only three years since, in 1967, William B. Skelton II, a nephew of William L., was elected to take his place.

The Company's financial progress since the sale of

Springfield was excellent. Earnings per share had improved almost every year. By 1965, which happened to be a down year, earnings per share were well over twice what they were before the sale of Springfield. In the earlier years of that eight-year time span, the Company benefited from the stock buy-back and the other securities purchased with the Springfield proceeds, but the municipal bonds were gradually sold as the acquisition program progressed. The real key was that under the leadership of Fletcher Means, ably assisted by John White and John Russell, the Company was honing its ability to realize optimum returns from its utility investments. The continuing cycle of plant expansion and improvements, followed by new financings and then another rate case, continued unabated.

Fletcher Means should also be credited with the initiation of Consumers' management style which differed from that of both Vernon West and the other multi-state holding companies in the industry. Vernon West had tended to be autocratic and, given his outstanding knowledge of the nuances of the industry, preferred to call the shots from Portland. Fletcher, however, realized that in spite of frequent visits to the subsidiaries, the Portland office could not possibly appreciate everything that was going on at the subsidiary level. His solution was to hire and nurture as high quality managers as each subsidiary could afford and grant them a wide latitude of local authority and discretion. That, of course, had to be tempered with the use of "superintendents" at the smaller subsidiaries, but all the larger subsidiaries during Fletcher's reign were run by either a resident president or a "Vice President and General Manager." (If not resident, the president would be a Consumers officer in Portland.) Fletcher also expanded, if not introduced, a system whereby the larger subsidiaries would have a board of directors, the majority of which consisted of local businessmen rather than appointees from the Portland office. That system provided excellent two-way communications. The local directors would advise and support the general manager on how to deal with the local politics and public relations in general, and they, in turn, by virtue of their participation in the management of their local water company, had a clear understanding of what the utility was attempting to accomplish and could articulate that knowledge to other influential people within the community. While water utility rate decisions should be based primarily on the technical merits of the case filed, there is no escaping the fact that rate decisions are influenced by local opposition, or a lack thereof, and the better a community appreciates what its water utility is doing, the less the utility will be faced with a hue and cry when it applies for increased revenue. Thus, the steady progress in earnings from 1957 to 1965.

The year 1965 did not mark the end of Consumers' acquisition program, but it did mark the completion of a replacement of the loss of Springfield. During the same period since the sale of Springfield, the Company also had adopted a policy of acquiring, whenever possible, small utilities in the general area of its operating subsidiaries. Those systems were either immediately connected to their larger neighbor or operated as "satellites" until natural expansion enabled the two utilities to interconnect. Thus, with normal growth and the aggressive acquisition program, by the end of 1965, Consumers' consolidated net plant was almost 5% greater than before the Springfield sale. The Company then owned and operated thirteen water utilities in seven states (including Shenango's Ohio subsidiary, Masury Water Company).

CHAPTER SEVEN

A New President and a Big Merger

By the 1966 annual meeting, Fletcher W. Means was ready to slow down. He had ably served the Company for thirty-eight years. Fortunately, the Company had two experienced younger men, John W. L. White and John J. Russell, either one of whom would make an excellent President. The board elected John White to fill the slot while Fletcher Means assumed a new title, Chairman of the board.

Although not President the entire time, Fletcher Means had run the Company for almost fifteen years, from May 1951 through December 1965. The financial progress of the Company over that time period was nothing less than spectacular. Granted, the Springfield sale doubled the book value of the Company's stock; but, in the fifteen years, the market value far more than doubled. In 1956 and every year from 1959 forward, in addition to the cash dividends the Company also declared stock dividends ranging from 4% to 10%. After adjustment for those stock dividends, during those fifteen years the book value per share increased six times over, from $5.05 per share to $31.79 per share. The cash dividend (also adjusted) was reinstated in 1955 at $.40 per share and increased every year to $1.20 per share in 1965. The market price (also adjusted) increased from less than $2 in 1950 to $47 in 1965.

John W. L. White, Consumers' fourth president, who was an employee and/or director for 50 years.

John White's management style was quite similar to that of Fletcher Means. The Company continued to emphasize decentralized management, "progressive water service," i.e., constantly anticipating future needs, and a vigilant search for new acquisitions. While the Springfield franchise provided a window every five years for the city to take over its water system, virtually all Consumers' other systems were, pursuant to state laws, subject to take-over by eminent domain proceedings at any time. Thus, the Springfield experience imbued a feeling that the best way to both survive and grow would be to continually search out and seize opportunities for new acquisitions to offset any unexpected takings.

After acquiring five utilities in 1964 and 1965, the next two years provided no further opportunities. However, three more utilities were added in 1968, namely **Oakland**

"Big Alice," an Allis Chalmers steam pump at Phillipsburg, N.J., is pictured above. When acquired by Consumers, the 1913 vintage pump was still operative on a stand-by basis.

Water Company in Maine for cash, **Sayre Water Company** on the Susquehanna River just south of the Pennsylvania—New York border, and **Peoples Water Company** in Phillipsburg, New Jersey, a short way downstream from the Delaware Water Gap. The Peoples acquisition was especially gratifying since it was the largest acquisition since the sale of Springfield, and it had been won against a competitive proposal by Elizabethtown Water Company, a large, highly respected water utility company headquartered in that state. As with most of the Sayre acquisition, Peoples was purchased through an exchange of Consumers 5% preferred stock. It is not certain whether the Peoples shareholders opted for the Consumers proposal because of a

larger cash dividend or a preference for Consumers' management style, or both. With over 6,500 customers, Peoples
became Consumers' third largest utility, exceeded only by
Shenango and Kankakee.

One might ask how Consumers went about finding
potential acquisitions. The managers of all the subsidiaries
had standing instructions to keep their eyes and ears open
as they participated in local (state) water utility functions.
In addition, both the corporate headquarters officers and
the larger subsidiary managers always attended the annual
meeting of the National Association of Water Companies.
There are two especially active national water utility associations. The largest is American Water Works Association
(AWWA) which is open to all water utilities, be they municipal or investor-owned. AWWA focuses primarily on hard-
ware, technology, and day-to-day operations. The other is
the National Association of Water Companies (NAWC)
which is open only to investor-owned water utilities which
make up only 20% of the water utility industry. The empha-
sis of NAWC is on finance, regulation (primarily rates), and
legislation.

Consumers' technical people, mostly engineers, regularly participated in both state and national AWWA affairs.
Consumers' corporate officers, major subsidiary managers,
and key financial personnel focused primarily on NAWC.
At those annual conferences, which are generally quite
intense and not a lark away from home, Company orders
were, again, "keep your eyes and ears open for potential
acquisitions." Besides those efforts, in the late '60's and
early '70's, Consumers retained a freelancing consultant,
James Corey, who was commissioned to ferret out potential
acquisitions. Jim was instrumental in finding all three New
Jersey acquisitions. Thus, various possibilities filtered up to

Consumers' senior management from a multitude of sources.

When John White assumed command in 1966, Consumers' decentralized philosophy had advanced to the point that there were two on-site Presidents. William T. Evans, a twenty-year veteran who at age eighteen had started as a laborer, was President of Shenango Valley Water Company. William D. Holmes, a registered engineer with ten years of experience at Kankakee, was President of Kankakee Water Company. In 1969, Robert H. Varney was moved up from General Manager to President of Camden and Rockland Water Company, and, a few years later, Gerald H. Lamprey, who had moved from the Portland office to New Jersey to manage the new acquisitions, was elected President of those merged properties, Garden State Water Company.

In 1969, Consumers purchased Westminster Water Company, a small utility in the suburbs of Erie, Pennsylvania. In the years that followed, several other small "developer" systems were purchased and interconnected with Westminster. The combined system was named **Erie Suburban Water Company**.

In March 1969, John J. Russell resigned his position and board seat to become an officer of Hannaford Bros., Inc., owners and suppliers of the largest food store chain in the state of Maine. John Russell and Hannaford's senior management had known each other well for several years. In 1961 the Company had decided to aggressively expand Dartmouth. The expansion included significant upgrading of virtually all its properties and the development of an industrial park in South Portland named Rumery Industrial Park in honor of Dartmouth's founder, Frank Rumery. The first company to locate in the Park was Hannaford

Bros. for whom Dartmouth built a nearly 200,000-square-foot warehouse. A few years later Hannaford expanded its facility and Dartmouth bought that property as well to lease back to Hannaford.

Eventually, in early 1969, management concluded that it had "too many eggs in Hannaford's basket." It sold all of the properties leased to Hannaford for an after-tax gain of approximately $400,000. From start to finish, John Russell had handled the negotiations. Hannaford was obviously impressed with both John's business acumen and his integrity. With virtually no opportunity for advancement at Consumers, John understandably elected to join the larger, rapidly expanding company. With his health failing, Fletcher Means resigned from the board later the same year.

The property improvements and Rumery Industrial Park required new equity to match Dartmouth's new mortgages. Since the Rumery heirs did not choose to increase their investment in Dartmouth, Consumers provided all the new equity capital. That moved Consumers' interest in Dartmouth from 50% to approximately 64%. Eventually, one by one, Consumers bought out the Rumery heirs, although the final 8% was not purchased until 1976.

John Parker, who had joined the Company in 1966 as an Engineer, was tapped to take over most of John Russell's duties. John had a Civil Engineering degree from Princeton and an MBA from Dartmouth and came to Consumers after twelve years with the Maine Central Railroad. He was soon elected Vice President, Secretary, and Treasurer.

In early fall of 1970, John White received a phone call extending an opportunity for the Company to purchase for cash a significant block of common stock and convertible debentures of **Ohio Water Service Company**. Consumers already owned a few shares of Ohio, but this would represent a large foot in their door. Ohio owned and operated six regulated municipal water utilities, all in the state of Ohio, and one unregulated water operation serving primarily steel mills in the Youngstown area. In all, Ohio was almost 80% the size of Consumers. The Company knew its management well since Ohio had always been deemed to be an ideal merger/acquisition target. Thus, Consumers had "courted" Ohio's officers regularly at NAWC meetings. Since the time for commitment before the securities would be shopped was short, an emergency board meeting was called. The cash required was a little less than $2 million. Both board approval and short-term credit terms were quickly obtained. The securities were purchased and, after the debentures were converted to common stock, Consumers had a 30% interest in Ohio.

In early 1971, over a time span of less than four weeks, an active director and two former presidents died. The first was Al Hauptfuhrer who had become a director with the acquisition of Hamilton Square Water Company. Three weeks later, the Company's founding President, Vernon West, died, and less than a week after that, the Company's second presiding manager and third President, Fletcher Means, died. To replace Al Hauptfuhrer, John Parker was elected to the board at the 1971 annual meeting. A year earlier, another new member had been added to replace Fletcher Means. William B. Russell, a son-in-law of former Maine Governor, Horace A. Hildreth, was elected to represent that family's interests.

Around this same period, Consumers lost one Maine utility and acquired another. In 1970, under the threat of condemnation, Consumers sold Winterport Water Company to a district formed to acquire that property. In 1971,

Consumers seized an opportunity to purchase for cash
Kezar Falls Water Company.

An update on the status of the Dartmouth Company is
appropriate at this time. Just as Dartmouth had enhanced
Consumers' cash flow from operations from the end of the
war to the sale of Springfield, so did Dartmouth continue
to contribute in the years following the Springfield sale.
The upgrading of Dartmouth's properties and the creation
of Rumery Industrial Park in the early '60's did require
supplemental funding from Consumers, but once that was
done, the pay-back was significant. The building, renting,
and eventual sale of the Hannaford Bros. warehouse established a pattern that would be repeated many times over
for the next twenty-five years. As properties were sold,
funds would become available to both purchase new properties and pay dividends to the parent company. Thus,
Dartmouth was continuously acquiring, improving, and
leasing properties throughout the Greater Portland area
and, at opportune times, selling them to enable the purchase of other properties. The only problem was that after
booking annual depreciation, Dartmouth's "Income from
Operations" was negligent in relationship to its net worth,
a negative insofar as Consumers' consolidated financial
reporting was concerned. But much of the financial community did eventually come to both understand and appreciate the value of Dartmouth. In the late '60's through the
early '80's, Consumers was able to report a gain from the
sale of property almost every year and, thus, for Consumers
and few other companies, "capital gains" were widely rec-
ognized as ordinary income and not discounted as a flash-
in-the-pan.

Consumers' investment in Dartmouth took a big step
forward in 1970. That year, through an exchange of stock,

Consumers acquired the P.H. and J.M. Brown Company, a closely held, Portland-based real estate investment company. The properties of P.H. and J.M. Brown were quickly transferred to the Dartmouth Company in exchange for additional Dartmouth stock. Among other advantages, the enlarged portfolio made it easier for Dartmouth to realize a property sale almost every year.

Following the acquisition of the 30% block of Ohio, Consumers' management quickly stepped up the courtship of Ohio's management. While the relationship remained friendly, the Ohio people were not about to roll over and play dead. They valued their independence and, understandably, they were out to get the best possible terms for their shareholders. But the tenacious and persuasive style of John White eventually won them over. Ohio and Consumers common stock had been selling at approximately the same price, $24 per share. However, Ohio's price was only 70% of book value while Consumers' was about 85% of book value. Thus, Consumers could afford a premium exchange ratio which was eventually set at $1\frac{1}{3}$ shares of Consumers for each share of Ohio. On a market basis, that was a 33% premium, but on a book value basis less than a 10% premium. Consumers' dividend rate was well below Ohio's, but because of the $1\frac{1}{3}$ exchange ratio, Ohio shareholders would enjoy a dividend increase of almost 10%. Both companies would benefit from improved market action and inherent economies of scale. With Consumers decentralized style, Ohio would also continue to operate quite independently with its own President and mostly local people on its board of directors.

While the 30% block of Ohio stock was bought in October 1970, it was not until early 1972 that the agreement in principle was negotiated. Then more time elapsed, primarily due to difficulties in gaining IRS approval of a tax-free exchange. The 30% block for cash was muddying the waters. Eventually a "triangular merger" was approved, i.e., Ohio would be merged into a newly formed Ohio subsidiary of Consumers. That took place on March 23, 1973. Because of the 30% cash purchase, the merger was accounted for as a "purchase" rather than the more common "pooling of interests" method.

But there was one benefit of the cash purchase. Because Ohio's prevailing stock price was so far below book value, the slight premium of the cash purchase was still well below book value. Further, that discount placed the overall acquisition at a slight discount from book value rather than a premium. Twenty-five years later, such terms would not be available for major acquisitions or aggressive mergers.

Thus, in 1973, Consumers almost doubled in size and more than doubled its number of shareholders (to over 3,000). Three Ohio directors came onto Consumers' board, namely, G. Taylor Evans, a past and long-time President of Ohio, Pierce Bailey, the then-President of the company, and James E. Mitchell, a long-time director and attorney for Ohio.

Since Ohio amounted to almost half of the size of the new Consumers Water Company, it is appropriate to summarize its history. The next chapter, which is derived primarily from a yet to be published history of Ohio Water Service Company written by its recently retired Treasurer, Stanley M. Massarelli, is intended to serve that purpose.

CHAPTER EIGHT

Ohio Water Service Company

I t is interesting to compare the history of Ohio Water
Service Company with that of Consumers Water Company. There are some striking similarities and some
significant differences. Like Consumers, Ohio was incorporated in 1926, only three months after Consumers. The
original name was Massillon Water Service Company, but in
early February 1928, the name was changed to Ohio Water
Service Company in anticipation of the consolidation of
several other Ohio water companies into that corporation.
Like Consumers, most of the utilities of Ohio Water Service
Company date back to well before 1926. The oldest Ohio
utility was the Massillon system which was started in 1853.
In fact, Massillon is probably the oldest utility in the entire
Consumers system.

This writer has a section of Massillon pipe mounted on

a board and dated circa 1853. It is wooden and was made from a 12-inch diameter log. While cast iron pipe dates back to the construction of Versailles and before, wooden pipe was very common in those days, especially away from the big cities. The wall of the pipe is 2 inches and, thus, the inside diameter approximately 8 inches. Sections of such pipe were normally 4 feet to 8 feet long and were bored by hand. The bore near one end would be enlarged slightly and the opposite end of log would be tapered. Thus, one section of pipe would be wedged into the next.

A story passed down about the start of the Wiscasset, Maine, system alleges that the town laid a wooden main from a lake some three or four miles distant, and, as soon as the ceremony to open the gate at the lake was completed, officials galloped their horses to a lather to ensure that they would reach town before the water. But, lo and behold, they had to wait over a week for the first trickle since it took that long for the joints to progressively swell enough to retain the inflow.

Unlike Consumers, Ohio was not started by a group of entrepreneurs. Rather, Massillon Water Service Company (subsequently Ohio) was a wholly owned subsidiary of Federal Water Service Corporation. Moreover, Federal Water Service was more than a water utility holding company in that, besides its nine water utility subsidiaries operating almost forty water systems in twelve states, it had extensive gas utility holdings. In recognition thereof, it eventually, in 1941, changed its name to Federal Water and Gas Corporation. But in 1926, Federal was one of, if not the largest and most extensive water utility holding company in the country. The other large water utility company at that time was American Water Works and Electric, the predecessor to American Water Works Company.

Like Consumers, Ohio Water Service Company experienced a period of acquisition and consolidation from 1926 to 1930. The first utility acquired by the new company was **Massillon Water Supply Company** in which Federal had only recently gained a controlling interest. The Supply Company authorized the sale of its assets to the Service Company the same day that Massillon Water Service Company was organized.

The next utility acquired was **Marysville** in February 1928. Federal had apparently gained control of Marysville in 1927. Two months later, on April 12, 1928, Ohio Water Service purchased all the assets of Mahoning Valley Water Company which had come under Federal's control a few years earlier. That Mahoning Valley system included a treatment plant adjacent to Burgess Lake and would subsequently be identified as Ohio's **Struthers** Division. Burgess Lake was named after Phil Burgess, the same engineer from Columbus who was one of the seven founders of Consumers.

At the end of April 1928, Ohio purchased, by the issuance of its own first-mortgage bonds, preferred stock and common stock to third parties, both the **Washington Court House** system and the Circleville system.

Finally, in April 1929, Ohio purchased from three families all the assets and rights of Trumbull and Mahoning Water Company. This system was designed to deliver untreated water to the steel mills in the Mahoning Valley and was subsequently called the **Mahoning Valley** Division. Two dams and reservoirs came with the Trumbull and Mahoning Water Company and, subsequently some of the dams and reservoirs of the original Mahoning Valley Water Company were transferred to the untreated and unregulated Mahoning Valley Water System.

As with Consumers, there were no further acquisitions for Ohio through the Depression and World War II. During the Depression, however, Ohio had an even tougher time than Consumers. By 1932 Ohio was unable to pay dividends on either its preferred or common stock. To the contrary, Federal was lending money to Ohio to keep it alive. By the end of 1934, Ohio owed Federal $1,333,000 on non-interest-bearing notes, and the preferred stock dividends were in arrears to the tune of $240,000. The next year, Ohio was forced to reorganize. All of the existing common and preferred stock was eliminated. A new class of common stock was created, two-thirds of which went to Federal in recognition of its unsecured notes while one-third went to the former preferred stockholders.

When Ohio Water Service was first formed, both its directors and officers were key officers of Federal Water Service Corporation. Stockholder and board meetings were normally held in New York at Federal's corporate headquarters. In 1932, however, the same year Ohio passed its dividends, Federal elected to abandon its centralized management. Contrary to Consumers' continuing policies, all of Federal's management contracts with its subsidiaries were terminated. A service company owned by the subsidiaries was formed to render support to the operating companies at cost. Federal would establish basic operating standards, but ongoing management was delegated to the subsidiaries. The President of Federal became board Chairman of the principal operating companies and other Federal officers remained on the subsidiary boards, but they could no longer serve as officers of the operating companies. One result of this change was that near the end of 1932, G. Taylor Evans was appointed District Manager serving Massillon, Washington Court House, Circleville, and

Marysville, and, in addition, was elected Assistant Secretary of the company. Ohio's main office was moved from Massillon to Struthers, and the next year, for the first time, the annual shareholders' meeting was held in Ohio. At that meeting G. Taylor Evans was first elected a director of the company and in 1936 he was also elected a Vice President of the company. By 1937 Mr. Evans was Vice President, General Manager and Treasurer of the company. Also rising through the ranks was J. Victor Carty who, in 1935, had transferred to Ohio Water Service Company from Federal's West Virginia subsidiary. He quickly rose from Accountant to Assistant Treasurer and, in 1937, was appointed Secretary of the company.

The Public Utility Holding Company Act, passed in 1936, had a significant impact on Ohio Water Service Company. Federal's gas interests were growing faster than its water utility business, and it was only a matter of time before Federal would have to divest its water utility holdings. After the reorganization of 1935, Ohio was able to resume its dividends, and, during the war, Ohio's Mahoning Valley Division more than doubled its revenues as the steel mills operated at peak capacity. By 1941, however, Federal had specific orders from the Securities and Exchange Commission to divest itself of its water utility holdings pursuant to the Public Utility Holding Company Act.

In December 1944, Ohio split its Class A common stock 3 for 1, and in April 1945, all of Federal Water and Gas Corporation's shares of Ohio were sold to the general public through an underwriting headed by Otis & Company of Cleveland. Upon completion, Ohio had 1,465 shareholders of which 429 were residents of Ohio. There were also many new shareholders from Pennsylvania and Maine, the former attributable to Claybough & Co. of Harrisburg and the latter believed to be attributable to Charles H. Gilman & Co. and H.M. Payson Co., both of Portland. At a reorganization meeting that month, all of the directors affiliated with Federal resigned, and a new slate of directors was elected that included representatives from each of the company's service territories. G. Taylor Evans was elected President and General Manager and retained his title of Treasurer. J. Victor Carty was elected Vice President and retained his title of Secretary. William R. Daly, who was President of Otis & Company, was elected Chairman of the board.

G. Taylor Evans was the most dominant figure in the history of Ohio Water Service Company. He had been Superintendent or General Manager of one or more of its operating utilities since well before the formation of the company in 1926 and had been the primary operating officer as the company was organized and progressed through the Depression and World War II. He ended up serving as President or full-time Chairman for almost twenty years (through December 1964) and was a director for forty-eight years, from 1933 to 1981. G. Taylor Evans was an even greater factor in the history of Ohio Water Service Company than Vernon West was in the history of Consumers, but the differences between the two are interesting to note. Vernon West was a true entrepreneur with a significant investment in his company while Taylor Evans had gone to work for an existing water utility and worked his way to the top without ever holding a significant amount of stock. Taylor Evans was a hands-on operating man well known by business leaders and politicians and hundreds of his customers throughout the Ohio Water Service system. One story has it that during the Depression Taylor would go door-to-door collecting bills so he could meet the payroll.

Another, indicating his no-nonsense character, reveals that he ordered the Mayor of Massillon's water turned off if he didn't pay his bill. On the other hand, Vernon West was a holding company man hundreds of miles from most of his operating companies and known only by a small number of people at each location. Vernon West tended to behave as if he owned all of the stock of his companies, whereas Taylor Evans was always conscious that he was a servant of both his customers and his shareholders. But servant that he was, once he became President, G. Taylor Evans became a strong leader.

The publicity of the forced divestiture by Federal Water and Gas of its water utilities created uncertainty in the municipalities served by Ohio Water. In Circleville, Massillon and Washington Court House, active campaigns for municipal acquisition were launched. The Washington Court House campaign soon fizzled out, while the citizens of Massillon voted down a proposal by a three to two margin. But at Circleville, the initiative was approved. That city had been agitating for the acquisition of its system since well before the mandated divestiture. It was finally sold in early 1947 for $420,000, a price set by a jury that resulted in only a modest gain of $61,000.

During the war, water supply had been a critical issue for both the Mahoning Valley industrial system and the Struthers domestic system. Pumpage was more than double that experienced during the Depression. Anticipating a solution as soon as the war ended, the company purchased extensive land for reservoirs in both the Berlin and Springfield water basins nearby. The more distant Berlin basin had by far the greatest potential, but all the company's holdings there were taken by eminent domain as the federal government developed a huge regional reservoir,

Berlin Lake. The Springfield project, however, was brought to fruition and created the largest reservoir in the Struthers-Mahoning complex, Lake Evans. That name was not just in honor of Ohio's new President but also in memory of Taylor's father and grandfather, both of whom had served in executive capacities for the predecessor company, Mahoning Valley Water Company. Lake Evans was completed in 1948 and enabled the company to derive approximately 50% of its revenues from the industrial system during the post-war boom.

As the company was planning and organizing systemwide improvements following fifteen years of Depression and war, it received another territorial setback. In 1947 the city of Campbell, which was served by the company's Struthers Division, refused to renew the company's franchise and eventually, with federal funds, built its own water treatment plant. (The plant did take its raw water from the company's Mahoning Valley Division.) The loss of Circleville and Campbell prompted the company to aggressively seek out added territory and new systems. In the Struthers area, the Mahoning Valley Sanitary District was expanding its territory at every opportunity. In the early 1950's the Struthers Division expanded its service area by obtaining contracts from Mahoning County for expansion into unincorporated areas. In 1956 the division laid a nine-mile extension into Boardman Township, initially to serve a new corporate headquarters for Youngstown Sheet and Tube Company. In 1959 the division expanded into North Lima, and in 1962 the division began serving the village of Lowellville.

At the same time the company was expanding its Struthers Division, it pioneered new territory to the north on the shores of Lake Erie. As early as 1947, the company

At right, G. Taylor Evans, the longest serving president and director of Ohio Water Service Co., at the 1948 dedication of the Mahoning Valley reservoir named in his honor. Above is the spillway of the new dam.

investigated the possibility of entering into the water business in both Lake and Ashtabula counties. At first the company's overtures were rejected, but eventually, in the Fall of 1955, the company contracted with the Lake County Commissioners and assumed operation of the county's small system immediately west of Painesville. The contract contemplated the company expanding and building a new intake into Lake Erie along with a modern water treatment plant. At a cost of $3 million, the company did precisely that, making the new **Lake Erie West** District the largest investment in the entire Ohio Water Service system. With the new plant, the company soon picked up the village of Mentor's municipal system and a franchise for a portion of the city of Willoughby. A few years later, in 1963, the company agreed to construct a distribution system in the village of Waite Hill.

The company's aggressive expansion resulted in an increase in Lake Erie West customers from 4,000 in 1955 to over 9,000 in 1962. The expansion, however, did not come without a price. The magnitude of the major investments in plant required increased rates, and the Company soon found itself in litigation with both Lake County and several of the municipalities served. In Ohio, water rates may be set by municipal ordinance, with an appeal to the Public Utilities Commission a measure of last resort. Much of the litigation began with disagreements over appropriate rates but eventually expanded into litigation over territories to be served. It was not until 1975 that all of the major disputes were settled.

Concurrent with the company's move into the Lake County-Mentor area, Ohio initiated water service twenty-five miles east in Ashtabula County. That business was started in December 1956, when the company acquired a small privately owned utility, Lake Shore Water Company serving 1,400 customers. The purchase was made by issuing 1,816 common shares valued at almost $50,000. Almost three years later, the company bought Lake County's water system in Madison Township, which abutted Ashtabula County to the East, and inter-connected the two utilities. The Madison system included a Lake Erie intake and a treatment plant and enabled the company to stop purchasing water from the city of Ashtabula. The customer count approximately doubled. In 1963 the company bought the city of Geneva's water system and extended mains to effect an interconnection. Shortly thereafter, water mains were extended south to and beyond Interstate 90 and from there, eventually, into the villages of Austenberg and Jefferson as well as Saybrook, Plymouth and Ashtabula townships. As with the Lake Erie West Division, the company's aggressive expansion at **Lake Erie East** resulted in extended litigation primarily over rates to support the company's huge capital expenditures and, to a lesser extent, over the company's right to serve in certain areas.

By the time Consumers entered the picture, in 1973, most of the litigation concerning territories at Struthers, Lake Erie West and Lake Erie East had been settled but, of course, for each of those three divisions, plus Ohio's other three divisions at Massillon, Washington Court House and Marysville, the impact of inflation and the need for continuing capital improvements required an endless series of negotiations for increased rates with the multitude of municipalities served.

In December 1964, G. Taylor Evans retired from full-time service. He had worked for Ohio Water Service Company since the day it was incorporated, always in a position of leadership.

Taylor continued as a director until his death in June 1981. His record of service and leadership is unmatched by anyone else cited in this book. Excluding his employment in predecessor companies, he had thirty-eight years of active service, nineteen years as CEO and forty-eight years as a director. Vernon West had the longest run as CEO, twenty-five years, but if you count one point for each year as (1) an employee, (2) a director, and (3) the CEO, Taylor Evans ranks #1, John White #2, and Vernon West #3.

J. Victor Carty was elected to replace Taylor Evans as CEO with the title of President. He had gone to work for Federal Water Service Corporation in 1931 and had been transferred to Ohio Water Service Company in 1935 to assume responsibility for the company's accounting and finance. Thereafter, he moved through the ranks steadily and had been elected a director of the company in 1960.

Vic Carty continued as President until his retirement at age 65 in 1969. In that year, G. Taylor Evans stepped down as Chairman, Vic Carty assumed that position, and Pierce Bailey was elected President. An engineer by training, Pierce Bailey joined the company in 1952, and, as he rose through the ranks, had served as Chief Engineer, Vice President of Operations, and Executive Vice President.

Thus, during the initial courtship by Consumers and subsequently during the serious negotiations, Victor Carty was serving as Chairman of Ohio's board and Pierce Bailey as President. Also active in the negotiations were G. Taylor Evans, still a director, and James E. Mitchell who had served as company attorney since shortly after World War II and a member of Ohio's board of directors since 1960.

CHAPTER NINE

The Balance of
John White's Legacy

The assimilation of Ohio Water Service Company into the Consumers system went quite easily. The cultures of the two companies had been fairly similar, and Consumers' decentralized policy meant that relatively few procedures at Ohio would be changed. At Ohio's next annual meeting, a few directors stepped down, but half a dozen continued to serve with only John White joining its board at the outset.

Ohio employees gained by the merger. Both Consumers and Ohio had formal retirement plans, but Consumers' was better. Initiated in the early '60's, Consumers' retirement package was a defined benefit plan, i.e., a function of years of service multiplied by an employee's average earnings of the last five years. Such a formula minimizes the impact of inflation over an employee's career. Ohio's plan, however, consisted of annuities purchased for each year of employment. Such a plan fails to recognize years of employment before adoption of the plan and renders annuities based on wages in the early years of employment quite meaningless as compensation increases due to both advancement and inflation. As with all companies acquired, Ohio employees were picked up by the Consumers plan which was well funded and able to absorb the past service liability. As a matter of fact, because Consumers' pension plan was so well funded and managed, there was a period of almost ten years in the mid-1980's into the early '90's during which there was no need for the Company to contribute additional cash in spite of steadily increasing wages. Credit for that outstanding performance goes primarily to the Company's Secretary since 1978, Brian R. Mullany. Brian guided the Retirement Committee of the board and recruited an outstanding money manager for the fund, W. P. Stewart & Co. Besides that, when interest rates peaked around 1980, it was Brian who suggested the fund withhold about $2.0 million from the money manager and purchase zero coupon bonds. About two years later, they were sold for a 100% profit. In fact, the unusual success with the retirement fund permitted Consumers to voluntarily increase the payout to those retired some seven or eight times between 1982 and 1995. The goal was to keep the benefits increasing at a rate equal to 50% of the inflation rate, and the Company pretty well succeeded. Such benevolence is extremely rare in private industry.

Over the years the water utility industry followed the lead of the power, gas, and telephone industries in providing favorable benefits for its employees. Consumers was no exception and, in a timely manner, instituted first an Employee Life Insurance Program and later an Employee Disability Program. Unique to Consumers was its Employee

The treatment plant at Kankakee. The newer portion, adjacent to the plant's source, the Kankakee River, was built in 1967 to house additional filters.

Savings Plan. John White believed in proprietary owner-ship and established a Company goal that every employee own some Company stock. To reach that goal, in 1966 Con-sumers' Savings Plan was initiated and, as savings were col-lected through payroll deduction, they were partially matched by the issuance of Consumers stock. That pro-gram continued until enabling tax legislation was passed to permit 401(k) programs. It was a simple matter to convert the Savings Plan to a 401(k) plan and, of course, the added benefit was that the savings then became pre-tax.

Consumers was also one of the first in the water utility industry to adopt an Employee Stock Option Plan. That was consistent with John's philosophy of employee stock ownership and was, therefore, quite broadly based and not excessively weighted to benefit just the top officers. John White was also responsible for the adoption of a broad-based, Key Employee Stock Bonus Plan.

The two years following the Ohio merger precipitated a fairly sharp drop in Consumers' earnings per share. EPS in 1973 were $2.64 (adjusted) and in 1975 were $1.49. That was the first year in which Consumers paid a cash dividend in excess of its earnings. That was done because the Company was jealously protecting an eighteen-year record of increased cash dividends (after adjustment for stock dividends), and it was reasonable to anticipate better earnings in the years ahead.

The decline in earnings was not due to the Ohio merger, although Consumers' involvement did not immediately solve Ohio's earnings problems. Rather, the problem was both companywide and industrywide. A frequently articulated advantage of Consumers Water Company was that because it was a multi-state utility company, when earnings go sour in one state, they are normally offset by better circumstances in the other states. But in 1975, earnings were bad in all states. The problem was threefold:

(1) inflation,

(2) increasing interest rates, and

(3) unresponsive regulation.

In the power and telephone industries, revenue growth was occurring without attendant and expensive increases in utility plant. Technology and economies of scale were winning the race against inflation. Since water utilities have always had the highest investment per revenue dollar of any type of utility, almost every batch of new customers required both main extensions and expensive increases in plant capacity. The rates were based on the historical cost of the utility plant, and since water utility plant is the longest-lived of any type of utility, replacement or augmentation of plant was at costs anywhere from two to ten times historical cost. When you combine those circumstances

with annual wage increases to keep up with current inflation and the refinancing of bonds at twice the historical
rates (remember the 3% and 4% bonds of the late '40's),
the need for higher rates without delay was critical.

Unfortunately, the public utility commissions in virtually all states failed to respond to the circumstances. They
were slow to understand why water utilities had to come in
for increased rates almost every year while their telephone,
power, and gas utilities were able to flourish with few if any,
rate increases and even offer rate decreases. Thus, water
rate cases of the mid-1970's normally endured from nine to
twelve months, were based upon the circumstances at or
before the date of filing and thus were totally inadequate
by the time they were allowed. Most commissions were slow
to accept "forward look" rate filings or similar measures
advocated by the industry to deal with its unique circumstances.

For Consumers the 1975 rate problem was compounded by the fact that the real estate market was not
conducive for a property sale and, thus, none was made
merely to generate a capital gain for Dartmouth.

Fortunately, management's and the board's confidence
in better times to come was well founded. In fact, for the
balance of John White's term as President, through 1983,
the Company posted an increase in earnings per share
each year. That, of course, enabled the Company to extend
its annual increase in dividends per share as well. However,
since small annual stock dividends create annoying cost
problems when shares are sold, the Company abandoned
that policy in 1979.

While earnings did turn up in the late '70's, the regulatory problems articulated above endured well into the
'80's. State commissions have a tendency to compare the

results of their decisions with those of other jurisdictions. As the Chairman of Elizabethtown Water Company used to say in those years, "comparing our financial circumstances with those of the rest of the water industry is like comparing our Company's health to a bunch of patients in a hospital." Market values for water utilities were chronically well below book value, decidedly unhealthy circumstances, especially when utilities are forced to raise additional capital to meet growing customer demands. To mitigate the circumstances, besides pursuing as aggressive a rate-making procedure as possible, Consumers was probably the most aggressive company in the industry to maximize customer advances and contributions in aid of construction. Advances and contributions provide "free" capital for new construction and thus minimize a utility's need to raise new and expensive capital of its own. That was especially beneficial in that period when short-term debt peaked out at 20% and long-term debt got as high as 13%. The requirement for advances or contributions of capital for construction is premised on the circumstances cited above that new construction is several times the average cost of existing plant. Thus, the utility would take the position that for a main extension to serve a new development, it would only invest per customer what its current investment per customer amounted to. To do otherwise would force existing customers to subsidize new development. Originally, that concept was based predominantly on the cost of water mains, but Consumers was aggressive in requiring "system development charges" as well to offset the inevitable investment in "backup plant," i.e., added wells or expanded treatment capacity. With such impact fees, combined with other sources of cash flow, the Company was able to limit net external financings to less than 25% of new utility plant constructed each year. By the end of 1983, the last full year of John White's tenure, customer contributions and advances aggregated over $28 million, almost 25% of the Company's net utility plant.

Aggressive main extension policies, however, were not enough. It is generally accepted that a water utility's capitalization ratio should be approximately 40% equity and 60% debt. In the years preceding the Ohio merger, Consumers' common equity ratio was hovering around 29% with another 8% or 9% of preferred stock. But Ohio was more heavily leveraged and, immediately following the merger, the combined common and preferred equity ratio was little over 31%. By 1975 that had dropped below 30%. For years, Consumers' market price had been well below book value, but for both the parent and the subsidiary companies to become financially strong, new equity capital had to be raised. Thus, in April 1977, for the first time in the history of the Company, Consumers issued common shares to the public for cash. You might say it was Consumers' IPO, but, of course, since its early years, and especially since 1930 when approximately 150 shareholders were picked up with the purchase of Springfield, Consumers had been issuing shares to the general public for acquisitions. This time, 125,000 shares were sold, with net proceeds just under $20 per share, to raise a little less than $2.5 million. McDonald and Company of Cleveland, Ohio, which for years had handled Ohio Water's financings, underwrote the offering with some sixteen other brokerage houses participating. That year, the combined equity ratio increased from barely over 30% to 34%. Because the proceeds per share were less than book value per share, the book value dropped from $26.35 to $25.51. This writer was intimately involved with the transaction and immediately thereafter made a personal vow to never again sell stock below book value (easier said than done if the market price is below book value). For the next five years the attrition of the Company's equity ratio was minimal, and in 1983, there was a major acquisition that gave the consolidated ratios a healthy boost. Also in 1983, but not affecting the equity ratio, was a two for one stock split.

The struggle to overcome or offset unresponsive rate regulation seemed endless and almost futile. Consumers was faring better than most of the industry, but for John White that was not enough. All sorts of approaches to enhance earnings and improve the stock price were explored. For several years, an aggressive program to sell under-utilized or idle assets was pursued. The most significant item was some 2,000 acres of open land in the Yankee Creek watershed near Ohio's Mahoning Valley Division. The land had been purchased in anticipation of yet another reservoir to supply the booming steel industry. But by 1950, the steelworker unions became too strong, and their demands gradually forced the mills to close. Besides having an adverse impact on Ohio's earnings, the closures also made it evident that there would never be a need for a reservoir on Yankee Creek. In this case, the first move was not to sell but rather contract with a gas company to drill wells and extract the gas that was known to be beneath the land. The Company would make no investment and there were high hopes for a bonanza of royalties. The bonanza, however, never materialized. Because Ohio had a pressing need for more capital and a ready buyer could not be found, the land was sold to Consumers at appraised value. It was eventually disposed of, but not all in one piece.

John White was also determined to maximize the profits of the Dartmouth Company and, beyond that, to explore possibilities for other diversification. Under the management of John Russell and subsequently Curtis M. Scribner, Dartmouth had always been managed conservatively and prudently. Dartmouth weathered the real estate slump of the mid-1970's with little trouble, and Curt Scribner was encouraged to undertake a few projects for immediate gain rather than long-term growth. In response, Dartmouth aggressively developed two garden apartment rental projects, and, after them, moved into the condominium development business.

To pursue further diversification, the Company initiated a few small-scale efforts, but eventually concluded that diversification would be effective only if a significant step was taken and, for that, outside help was needed. Thus, in late 1981, Consumers retained the consulting firm of Harbridge House, Inc. to assist both the management and the board in:

(1) deciding whether significant diversification was appropriate and, if so,

(2) determining what avenues would be most appropriate.

The process took over a year, but in early 1983 the Company announced an agreement in principle to purchase, through an exchange of stock, Burlington Homes of New England and Schiavi Homes, both located in Oxford, Maine. Burlington manufactured mobile and modular homes while Schiavi was a mobile home dealer selling Burlington and other brands of manufactured housing. The deal was closed by the end of March. Richard Ryan and John Schiavi were the principal stockholders of Burlington and John Schiavi the proprietor of Schiavi Homes. 225,000 (pre-split) common shares were issued, and both John Schiavi and Dick Ryan came on the board.

The Burlington Homes plant in Oxford, Maine

The companies were deemed to be a good fit with the Dartmouth Company, and Dartmouth formed a new subsidiary, The Arcadia Company, to develop projects for manufactured housing. The intent was to develop high-end mobile home parks plus modular housing projects, both consistent with the quality standards and image of Consumers Water Company.

Besides Messrs. Ryan and Schiavi, there were other new faces on Consumers' board. In 1976, because of his outstanding business expertise and his intimate knowledge of both the Company and the water utility industry, John Russell was persuaded to rejoin the board. In 1977, George Payson died and Bill Skelton decided not to stand for re-election. In 1978 Jack S. Ketchum, an independent financial consultant, and John E. Palmer, Jr., were elected to the board. Around 1970 John Palmer had managed the Dartmouth Company for almost a year, but, consistent with his statements when he was hired, he had left the Consumers organization to purchase and manage a business on his own. In 1980 Pierce Bailey died and the next year, both Ben Alexander and Taylor Evans, who by then were advisory directors, also died. That same year John E. Menario, former Manager of the city of Portland and then an independent consultant, was elected to the board. The Company was fortunate to attract such strong directors.

By the time Burlington and Schiavi were purchased, John White was in the process of stepping down. In 1981, a transition was announced with John White moving up to Chairman and CEO and John Parker being elected President and COO. That arrangement continued through 1983, and in 1984 John White retired and John Parker was elected President and CEO. To avoid any confusion over who was running the Company, John White was replaced as Chairman of the board by long-time director and attorney from Fryeburg, David R. Hastings.

It is interesting to compare the financial progress of the Company during John White's eighteen years of leadership with that of Fletcher Means' fifteen-year term. Because the industry was maturing and because there was no sale to double the value of the Company as the Springfield sale did, the numbers are not quite as spectacular. But, nevertheless, they are unusually good and led most, if not all, of the industry. As already stated, the annual small stock dividends were discontinued after 1978, but during John White's tenure, there were two stock splits, a 4 for 3 split in 1967 and a 2 for 1 split in 1983. The per share figures that follow are adjusted for those splits and the stock dividends. From 1966 through 1983, book value per share increased 70% from $9.25 to $15.71 while earnings per share from operations increased 203% from $.65 to $1.97. During the same period the market value increased over 120% from approximately $10 per share to a little over $22 per share. The strong growth in book value is attributable to the almost annual capital gains that came mostly from the Dartmouth Company and the resulting relatively low payout ratio. During the earnings dip around 1975, the payout ratio was high, but in both 1966 and 1983, the payout ratio was only a little over 50%. One of John White's objectives had been to keep the shareholders' position ahead of inflation. It was a tough environment in which to meet that goal since the CPI increased 214% during those eighteen years, but the cash dividend actually increased 244% and earnings per share increased 263%. It was a truly remarkable record during some very difficult circumstances.

Aggregate growth was equally strong. The Ohio merger was a big plus, but the aggressive expansion of each operating company through the purchase of satellites or other means over the years yielded significant results. The number of customers increased by 225% while the Company's net water utility plant increased over 363%. At his last annual meeting of shareholders before retirement in April 1984, John White held up a stock certificate he had been given by Vernon West approximately thirty-seven years earlier, soon after he went to work with the Company. He proceeded to advise the shareholders that when you include the stock splits and stock dividends that came from that certificate, its value had appreciated approximately fifty times over.

CHAPTER TEN

John Parker's Watch

The Company was in excellent condition when John White passed the baton to John Parker. In the new CEO's first Annual Letter to Shareholders, he was able to boast of Consumers' ninth consecutive year of increased earnings per share and the twenty-seventh consecutive year in which dividend payments to shareholders were increased. The record of increased cash dividends was the longest in the investor-owned water utility industry and among the top ten in the entire Over-The-Counter Market. Another increase in net income to almost $6 million was "especially significant since 1983 results included over $1 million of gains from sales of property while gains of 1984 amounted to only $124,000."

Contributing to that income gain was the first full year of Schiavi Homes Corp. and Burlington Homes of New England, Inc. The contract for their purchase included bonus shares based upon the performance of the two companies in their first three years of operation. Thus, Richard Ryan and John Schiavi not only monitored their progress closely but also assisted management greatly in their efforts to learn the new business. The Company's two lesser new areas of diversification were not doing quite as well. Arcadia was running into fierce opposition in seeking necessary permits for developing manufactured hous-

John van C. Parker, president from 1984 to 1992

ing communities, and a new joint venture with Malcolm Pirnie, Inc. (the same consulting engineering company that broke the deadlock over the location of a new reservoir for Springfield City Water Company) had yet to turn a profit. That venture was initially called Consumers-Pirnie Utility Services Company and was designed to offer a variety of services to both water and wastewater utilities, primarily municipally owned. That year two different proposals for privatizing municipal utility operations had been rejected.

The market for Consumers stock reflected the Company's progress. Of the eighteen publicly traded water companies, Consumers had the third highest market-to-book ratio, 1.51. That was a vast improvement over 1977 when the Company had to issue new stock below book value.

Consumers had been rising with the tide as industry circumstances improved, but under John White's leadership, the Company rose somewhat faster than the tide. John White deserves the credit for that. For his Retirement Party a booklet describing the success of his eighteen-year presidency was prepared without his knowledge. Among other topics, it outlined several characteristics of his management style whose headings were as follows:

(1) quiet mannered,
(2) modest,
(3) persistent,
(4) high ethical standards,
(5) loyalty to the Company,
(6) belief in personal motivation and proprietary ownership,
(7) knowledge of and attention to detail,
(8) concern for the individual,
(9) innovation,
(10) concern for the shareholder, and
(11) dedication to quality service.

Because it is unique, the elaboration of one of the above, concern for the shareholder, is included here. "There are probably few, if any, Chief Executive Officers of publicly traded companies who have had as much concern for the individual shareholders as John White. This applied to holders of just a few shares as well as those who held larger blocks. To John they were individuals, a portion of whose savings were committed to the Company. He took most seriously their trust and faith in the future of Consumers Water Company. Every new shareholder was written a personal letter welcoming the investor to the Consumers family. There were several standard forms for such letters, but each recipient was screened to determine whether the investor was either a friend of John White's or anyone else in the Company. For example, if a mailing address was in

Kankakee, Illinois, before writing, Bill Holmes, President of Kankakee Water Company, would be asked whether he or someone else in the company knew the individual. If the reply were positive, a personal touch would be added. Thus, it is not surprising that Consumers' family of share-holders is an unusually loyal one. One of the greatest frus-trations for John was the trend toward stock ownership in street name or common accounts for trust departments where the true identity of the beneficial shareholder is not available."

By 1984, the caliber of Consumers' key employees was, in the biased opinion of this writer, the best in the industry. With John White gone, John Parker needed help in Port-land, especially as to water utility operations. He persuaded the strongest subsidiary president, Bill Holmes, to move from Kankakee to Portland. Consumers had always had a policy of offering moves for advancement but refrained from penalizing if an individual declined. The Company's experience was that most out-of-state personnel viewed Portland, Maine, as the end of the world and, conversely, people at the corporate headquarters could not bear the thought of leaving the state of Maine. Bill Holmes was a big wheel in Kankakee, and his feelings about Portland were not atypical. Out of loyalty to the Company, however, he agreed to the move and was appointed Executive Vice Pres-ident–Water Utilities. Bill was also elected to Consumers' board. At the same time, John Isacke, who was an out-standing financial officer for the parent, was tapped to become Senior Vice President–Real Estate and Housing. A strong team was in place and the future appeared rosy.

Besides the diversification already cited, there was one other significant change in the Company's non-utility busi-ness. In 1982, Curtis Scribner resigned his presidency of the Dartmouth Company for a better opportunity in the same line of business. Before coming to Dartmouth, Curt had been a banker and, in spite of urgings from John White to generate "ordinary income," had managed Dartmouth in a conservative manner. F. Gordon Hamlin was hired to replace him. Gordon had a background of more aggressive real estate experience, primarily developing and selling syndications. He didn't need any push to change the style of Dartmouth's management.

In the decade of the '80's, regulation of water utility rates gradually improved. The passage of the National Safe Drinking Water Act was a benefit to the investor-owned segment of the industry (only 20%) because, in general, the larger private water companies were better managed and had better utility plants for both stricter standards and future growth. Nevertheless, because of the advantage of municipal ownership in the areas of taxation, finance, and government grants, there was always the threat of periodically losing properties through eminent domain proceedings.

To more than offset those losses, the Company continued to encourage aggressive searches for new companies and growth of its existing systems, including occasional purchases of satellites. Bill Holmes, and his successor Charles Smith, were the most successful in this area, and by the end of the decade had four small divisions besides Kankakee making up Consumers Illinois Water Company.

The first significant acquisition since the Ohio merger occurred in 1985. Early in the year, John Parker received a phone call from the Philadelphia law firm, Morgan Lewis and Bockius (ML&B) inquiring whether or not Consumers would be interested in purchasing **Roaring Creek Water Company** of Shamokin, Pennsylvania. Of course there was

A view of the 12,000-acre watershed at Roaring Creek. The large pile of coal mine tailings just above the town is below the company's intake. With modern techniques the slight amount of anthracite in the tailings, known as culm, can be economically recovered. Thus, ever since Consumers bought the company, the material has been gradually sold.

interest, and within a week he and Harold E. (Ed) Woodsum of the Company's primary law firm, Drummond Woodsum Plimpton and MacMahon, journeyed to the Philadelphia law offices. There they were told that the principal owner and president, Doug McWilliams, was in failing health, had no heirs interested in running the company, and, therefore, wished to dispose of the utility in an orderly manner. Consumers was granted the first opportunity to propose. This was somewhat of a surprise since the other two water utility holding companies, American and General, were headquartered in or near Philadelphia and were far better known to both the law firm and the owner than Consumers.[6] Nevertheless, when Mr. McWilliams laid out his criteria for a sale, in the law firm's considered opinion, Consumers stood at the top of the list. The two primary considerations were an owner who would give first-class water utility service to the area and an attractive stock available for a tax-free exchange. At the meeting, John and Ed were told that if Consumers' proposal were sufficiently attractive, they would shop no further. John and Ed returned with an armful of data, and within a few days a proposal was made subject to Consumers' board approval and a due diligence inspection of the company's property, books, and records. The proposal was acceptable and, shortly thereafter, John and Bill Holmes went to Shamokin to inspect the property. The water source for Roaring Creek was an absolute jewel. Between two parallel ridges of the Pennsylvania Allegheny Mountains, Roaring Creek owned 12,000 acres in which there were two large reservoirs and a lower impoundment for the collection, chlorination, and pumping of the unfiltered water. The company owned every square foot of the watershed with the exception of a state highway that crossed the valley near the top. It was entirely wooded and, besides the intake structure, the only buildings were three company-owned homes. The pumping and distribution system was adequate although there was evidence that the company had not been aggressive in its extension policies.

There was one unusual feature of one of the reservoirs. John noticed that a large percentage of the shoreline was

---

[6] John White reports that many years earlier Fletcher Means had "cultivated a relationship with the McWilliams family."

stone lined, obviously the fruit of thousands of manhours of manual labor. Upon inquiry, he was told that during the Depression when customers could not pay their bills, they worked them off by collecting rocks in the adjacent woods and placing them along the water's edge to minimize silting.

Just as unique as the watershed and reservoirs was the situation with the company dams. Some ten years earlier, Hurricane Agnes had dumped record-breaking rainfalls that had threatened, but failed to breech, the two major dams. Immediately thereafter, the company repaired what damage was done and reconstructed the spillways to meet modern federal standards for dam construction. A few years later, however, as a result of two or three isolated dam failures in other areas of the country, the federal government issued yet stricter and more demanding dam specifications with a mandate that existing dams must be upgraded to meet the higher standards. Thus, having spent $2 or $3 million following Hurricane Agnes, the company was now about to let contracts totaling $5 or $6 million to rebuild the spillways all over again. While that would strain Consumers' overall capital budget in the next two years, the Company proceeded with the acquisition undaunted.

In hindsight, there was only one negative aspect of the entire affair. The agreement in principle, quickly signed by both parties, allowed for a more definitive contract before the closing, a normal procedure for such an acquisition. The lesson subsequently learned for Consumers was to demand in such circumstances that the selling company's legal expenses be paid for by its shareholders rather than the company or, alternatively, to place a cap on what the selling company could expend. The definitive contract was handled by ML&B's Harrisburg office, and the attorney involved seemed to make a career annuity from the task. Thus, legal nitpicking went on for almost ten months, and since the ML&B charges went to Roaring Creek, Consumers ended up paying both sides of the legal hassle.

Roaring Creek also provided an opportunity for Consumers to demonstrate one of its more beneficial attributes, regrettably almost totally unappreciated by state public utility commissions in their regulatory process. Consumers' Chief Engineer, Paul Noran, called for an immediate hold on the letting of dam reconstruction contracts. The specifications had been drawn up by one of the country's leading engineering firms for that discipline and were little different from what any other consulting firm would have recommended. But Paul Noran was an expert in value engineering. He thoroughly reviewed the new federal specifications and, after working with the consulting engineers, came up with revised designs and specifications that would meet the federal standards yet cut the costs by approximately one-third. Overall dam safety was not compromised. After all, even before the recent reconstruction, the dams had survived a once-in-a-hundred-years rainfall. Thus, the second go-around of Roaring Creek's dam reconstruction was accomplished with a saving of some $2 million.

Several years later, Roaring Creek was the victim of still more regulatory overkill. The water utility serving the Scranton-Wilkes Barre area in the mid-1980's had two or three watersheds similar to Roaring Creek's from which they drew and delivered untreated water with the exception of chlorination. One summer over a long weekend, one of the utility's chlorinators failed, and the system received large quantities of unchlorinated, raw water. The net result was that a few dozen customers came down with giardia, which comes from an organism that gets into water primarily from beaver feces. There are several ways to prevent such an occurrence, including alarm systems for the chlorinators if they fail and comparatively inexpensive detention chambers to ensure adequate contact time for the chlorine before any water reaches a consuming customer. But while nobody died from the incident, the Scranton outbreak became a political football, the net result of which was that Pennsylvania passed a law overriding the federal Safe Drinking Water standards. Federal standards allow exceptions to the general rule to filter if circumstances so warrant. The new Pennsylvania law mandated full water treatment and filtration for all public water supplies utilizing surface water sources regardless of how pristine their watershed. Thus, some ten years after acquisition, Roaring Creek was required to spend $16 million for a new complete water filtration plant. In contrast, two well-known water systems in Maine, Portland Water District and Consumers' Camden and Rockland system, were able to qualify for the exception to the federal mandate.

Meanwhile, there were several other acquisitions and sales during the 1980's. In 1984, the **University Park** utility, some twenty-five miles north of Kankakee, was purchased. Then, the year after Roaring Creek was purchased, another significant acquisition occurred, namely, the purchase of **Inter-State Water Company**. Bill Holmes had been courting Inter-State for years without success, but finally the owners contacted Bill and indicated they were ready to sell. Inter-State serves Danville, Illinois, adjacent to the Indiana border approximately one hundred miles south of Kankakee. The next year, 1987, Kankakee also acquired the utility serving a recreational area known as **Woodhaven**. An interesting feature of Woodhaven and University Park was that both water utilities came with the area's wastewater utility as well. A few years earlier, a small Kankakee satellite also came with a wastewater facility. Thus, Consumers' Illinois management team was gaining expertise in sewage treatment as well as water treatment. Also coming with a waste water system in Illinois was the **Candlewick** water utility purchased in 1988. The last Illinois acquisition was **Oak Run** water utility acquired in 1989.

On the disposition side, all under the threat of condemnation, Newport was sold in 1980, Wilton in 1983, the Wiscasset system in 1984, and the Erie Suburban system in 1985. While Consumers was not anxious to sell any of these systems, they all sold at a profit, and the Erie Suburban sale was especially rewarding. Erie served only 2% of Consumers' customers, had been a subsidiary for only sixteen years, yet generated a gain after taxes of $1.9 million, by far the largest gain since the sale of Springfield. Much of the gain was attributable to a high percentage of contributed property. A utility is not allowed to earn on contributed property, but if the property is taken involuntarily, it does belong to the utility company, and the company is entitled to fair compensation.

That characteristic of the business led to a second unsuccessful hostile take-over attempt. In the Spring of 1981, New Zealand-based Industrial Equity (Pacific) Ltd. filed with the SEC, as required by law, a form indicating that they held over 5% of the Company's stock. Industrial Equity was one of several companies controlled by Robert Brierley, a well-known corporate raider in Australia. His modus operandi, sometimes called rationalization, was to purchase a company, split it up into several parts, and sell them for a tidy gain. His idea was to gain control of Consumers and then sell off the subsidiaries for a handsome profit. There were, however, two problems. First, he was unable to get much more than 10% of the Company's shares without driving up the stock price beyond an acceptable level. Second, at that time it was only a condemning municipality that would be willing or forced to pay multiples of book value for a water utility. Ordinary investors would only pay an amount consistent with what public utility commissions would allow the properties to earn. Most municipalities are content with their investor-owned water utilities and, thus, there was no way Industrial Equity would be able to liquidate Consumers at the multiples of book value he anticipated. After two years, and the attendance at an annual meeting of a representative of Industrial Equity, Mr. Brierley realized the facts of life and Industrial Equity's holdings were liquidated.

A few years later, in February 1986, another major shareholder appeared on the scene. Almost all the shares that Consumers had issued in exchange for Schiavi Homes and Burlington Homes of New England were sold to Compagnie Generale des Eaux (CG), the largest water utility company in France. CG, however, was no corporate raider. It felt that the United States was an attractive place to invest excess funds and was anxious to exchange technical expertise in the interest of improving both French and American water companies. Among other companies in which CG was investing was Philadelphia Suburban Water Company that served a multitude of municipalities surrounding Philadelphia. CG accumulated more than 15% of Consumers' stock, and in 1987 a representative of the company, Jean Claude Banon, was elected to Consumers' board.

The years following 1975 were the golden years for Consumers Water Company. Except for fluctuations in capital gains, earnings and earnings per share increased consistently. By 1988, earnings per share from operations alone had increased eight consecutive years, and total earnings per share were at a record high, except for 1957 when Springfield was sold and 1985, the year of the Erie Suburban sale. 1988 also marked the thirty-second consecutive year of increased payout to shareholders and the tenth consecutive year of significant capital gains which averaged $620,000 per year. That year the Company was honored by the Maine Chapter of the Newcomen Society of the United States, and John Parker had a wonderful story to tell.

But there were some clouds on the horizon. In the mid-1980's, the real estate markets were booming, and the new aggressive policy for Dartmouth led that subsidiary to accelerate its program of condominium developments. Besides several projects in the Portland area, in 1986 Dartmouth purchased two ongoing condominium developments at the Sugarloaf Mountain Ski Resort in northwestern Maine. Sugarloaf was struggling financially and headed toward bankruptcy. The next year, 1987, Dartmouth sold sixty-three condominiums including twenty-four at Sugarloaf. That same year, Dartmouth bought three other Sugarloaf condominium projects that had all the necessary approvals but had not been started. They were purchased at distressed prices, as Sugarloaf filed for bankruptcy, and positioned Dartmouth as the sole real estate developer on the mountain.

In the mid-1980's, the Arcadia Company and C/P Utility Services Company also gained new status. In 1986 Arcadia was spun off from Dartmouth and became a direct subsidiary of Consumers. Stanley R. Goodnow was hired as President of Arcadia, and shortly thereafter Arcadia was heavily involved with a 221-unit manufactured housing development in Taunton, Massachusetts, and a 100-unit project in Windham, Maine. In 1987, after almost four years of growing revenue but no profits, Malcolm Pirnie Inc. decided it had had enough. Initially, Consumers felt the same way, and plans were made to liquidate the company. At the last minute, however, C/P picked up what appeared to be an attractive contract, the net result of which was that Consumers bought out Malcolm Pirnie's interest in C/P. 1987 also saw a change in the presidency at Burlington Homes. That, combined with a changing market that required revised production techniques, resulted in reduced volume and lower earnings for Burlington.

Meanwhile, Consumers had become disillusioned with Schiavi Homes, the retailing operation. To be a successful retailer, Schiavi had to offer a full line of mobile and manufactured housing which would include some brands of low-cost, low-quality mobile homes. Such products simply did not fit well with the high quality image Consumers strove to project. That, combined with an unsuccessful turnover in the presidency of Schiavi, led Consumers to sell Schiavi in 1986. In hindsight, the timing could not have been better. The company was sold to the Penobscot Indian tribe that had recently won a huge award through an Indian land claim suit. The gain on the sale was $426,000, and Consumers' compound average annual return on its investment in Schiavi since acquisition amounted to 20%.

The peak year of 1988 was attributable to an unusually strong year for the water subsidiaries. Inflation was down, interest rates were reasonable, rate decisions were better, and summer sprinkling loads were high. The clouds were over the non-utility side of the business, recently labeled the Enterprise Group. Burlington continued to suffer production problems while unit sales and earnings for both Dartmouth and Arcadia were down due to a weakening market. The only bright spot was that, for the first time, C/P Utility Services made a profit. That was due in a large part to the contract secured as Consumers bought out Malcolm Pirnie. C/P was named to operate in the upper Delaware River basin a huge pump storage project known as Merrill Creek and designed to maintain adequate flows in the Delaware during dry summer months. The construction was financed by some eight or ten power companies that drew cooling water from the Delaware downstream, but they chose to have a third party operate the facility.

In 1988 two directors terminated their board service. At the annual meeting, John McInnes requested that he not be re-appointed an Advisory Director, a status he had held since 1976 because of the Company's policy on age. In all, John had served on the board for forty-four years, by a wide margin the longest service of any Consumers director. He had always been a constructive and valuable participant and a pleasure to work with. For many years, as a partner at H.M. Payson Co., he had managed Consumers' Retirement Plan portfolio most successfully. This writer will always remember one remark he made: "You'll never get any big fish unless you go out where the sharks are." Of course, for a retirement fund portfolio, he never went after the big fish, but his management of the portfolio had been excellent. Near the end of that same year, Richard Ryan asked that he not be re-nominated because of pressing business interests. Dick had been most helpful in educating Consumers' management as to the nuances of the manufactured housing business.

In 1989 the clouds became darker, figuratively for Dartmouth and Arcadia and literally for the water utilities. For the latter, in contrast to 1988, it was a very wet summer for almost all of them. Compounding their problems, while major construction, precipitated in part by the Safe Drinking Water Act, was underway, short-term interest rates were up again. After relatively quiet years in 1987 and 1988, almost all the subsidiaries were in for increased rates and, once again, regulatory lag became a problem.

But the Enterprise Group had bigger problems. Unit sales for both Arcadia and Dartmouth were way down and at a level that could not carry the millions of dollars of borrowed funds invested in their various projects. On a combined basis, those two subsidiaries lost over $850,000. It was the Company's first decline in operating earnings since 1975. Dartmouth was involved in the worst real estate crisis since the Depression. It was a rude awakening, and before year-end, both management and the board concluded that the earnings of the real estate business during the "golden years" had not been sufficient to offset the adverse impact of bad years, at least for a publicly traded water utility company like Consumers. In the Spring, the Company announced that it would phase out of the real estate development business. That year Sugarloaf Mountain Corporation was aggressively looking for a buyer, and all of Dartmouth's projects at Sugarloaf were included in the offering prospectus. Curiously, Burlington finally solved most of its production problems and had a better year in spite of a bad year for its industry. In addition, C/P had a record year with net income comparable to some of the largest water utilities, but with only a fraction of their investment.

In 1990 the roof fell in. The real estate losses were so bad that in July the Company announced that it was quitting the real estate business completely. That precipitated so-called "discontinuance accounting" which meant that a reserve was immediately booked for all anticipated losses of Dartmouth and Arcadia through to their complete liquidation. Initially, a reserve of $4.3 million was booked, Consumers' entire investment in Dartmouth and Arcadia. By year-end it was realized that significant other expenses would be incurred as well, and the reserve was increased to $8.9 million. When it was all over, the next year, part of that was reversed and the eventual loss was $7.1 million. Gordon Hamlin resigned from Dartmouth and Stan Goodnow took over the most demanding and delicate assignment of liquidating the companies.

Of the multitude of investments, some were under water and some had residual values net of their mortgages. Rather than take the second write-off of $4.6 million, Consumers could have elected to have Dartmouth declare bankruptcy and walked away from it all. But that would have tarnished Consumers' reputation nationally and spoiled many strong business relationships. Some of the financial institutions that had mortgages greater than the real estate values threatened to precipitate bankruptcy or, alternatively, seek recourse from Consumers' deep pockets. But Stan Goodnow, with excellent assistance from attorneys Dan Amory of Drummond and Woodsum and George Marcus, convinced them that:

(1) they could not pierce Consumers' "corporate veil," and
(2) they would be far better off allowing him to process an orderly liquidation than initiating an expensive bankruptcy proceeding.

When the liquidation was completed the next year, well ahead of schedule, all the creditors came out whole (a far cry from many of the bank's other investments) and, as already stated, Consumers was able to reverse $1.8 million of the booked reserve. Stan had done an outstanding job.

It is interesting that both Consumers' acquisition and Consumers' loss of Dartmouth were precipitated by real estate crashes. How could the two crashes have such diametrically opposed results for the same company? The basic difference was that in the '30's, Consumers was owned and managed by a group of entrepreneurs who harbored few feelings about having to answer to other shareholders, were not earnings per share conscious, and were willing to take some risks. But in 1990, Consumers was a publicly traded company with over 3,800 shareholders acutely conscious of earnings per share and their regular dividends. Further, with the huge capital requirements mandated by the Safe Drinking water Act, the Company had to maintain an acceptable stock price for the more than likely possibility of another common stock offering for additional equity capital.

Thus, the best course was to bite the bullet, chalk off 1990 as a dismal aberration and get on with the water utility business. Never mind that Consumers could no longer boast of its "treasure house of unrealized values" or claim that it was "not just another utility." With one exception, the balance of Consumers' business was also bad in 1990. It was another year of heavy rainfall, rate decisions were coming in behind schedule, and Burlington's earnings were down again. Moreover, at Southern New Hampshire (formerly Hudson Water Co.), that subsidiary experienced significant losses because of huge investments necessary to bring several recently acquired satellite systems up to acceptable standards consistent with the Safe Drinking Water Act. The bottom line was that the Company booked only $1.09 per share from on-going operations, a $.12 per share gain from a sale of Wanakah, and a $1.54 per share loss from Dartmouth and Arcadia. The net loss of $.33 per share was the first and only year's loss in the history of the Company. Nevertheless, jealously guarding its unique record, the Company increased, modestly, its dividend payout for the thirty-fourth consecutive year. In that regard, Consumers was in the elite top 1% of all publicly traded companies.

In 1990 Consumers lost three directors. CG transferred Jean Claude Banon from New York to London, and Claudio Elia took his place. CG's holdings were up to 20%, and they continued to be a supportive partner. Because of failing health, John Russell resigned. With a short break after he terminated employment with the Company, he had served on the board for twenty-five years and had been an extremely valuable director. And because of mounting age, Jim Mitchell, who had been an Advisory Director for the past five years, requested that he not be re-appointed. Jim Mitchell had been a very helpful director for both Consumers and especially Ohio Water Service Company. While he was never an employee of Ohio, every President after Taylor Evans leaned heavily on Jim for both legal and business advice. Jim had been a key player in the aggressive expansions of the Struthers and the two Lake Erie districts.

Remarkably, the Company bounced back fast from the Dartmouth disaster. Net income in 1991 was the largest in the Company's history and, even on an earnings per share basis, was the largest since the sale of Springfield. The total earnings were boosted by the $1.8 million reversal of the Dartmouth liquidation reserve plus a $3.1 million gain from the sale of Ohio's Marysville Division which was taken under the threat of condemnation. Offsetting those gains was a not insignificant mandated write-down of Southern New Hampshire's rate base amounting to $600,000. The money Consumers had spent to bring the shoestring-designed developer systems into EPA compliance was deemed by the New Hampshire PUC to be excessive and more than the ratepayers could bear. If the systems were still in the hands of the developers, some other solutions would have been found, but for the New Hampshire PUC, over the years a normally fair commission, Consumers' deep pockets were too much to resist.

Capital expenditures reached a record level that year, $30 million. $14 million of that was attributable to a brand new 14 million gallon per day water treatment plant for Inter-State Water Company. Coincidentally, as the new plant was under construction the previous year, the 100-year old plant that it was replacing was flooded out by a once-in-a-hundred-year flood of the adjacent Vermillion River. It took five days to reinstate service, the worst break in service in Consumers' history. The new plant was being constructed on higher ground.

The Dartmouth fiasco, combined with the continuing dividend policy and the extraordinarily high capital expenditures, pushed Consumers' equity ratio well below acceptable levels. From 1988 to 1990, the ratio had fallen from 40% to 32%. Accordingly, for the second time, Consumers went to the open market for additional equity capital. Tucker Anthony, Inc. headed up the underwriting syndicate. This time the terms were far more favorable. Fortunately, the losses of 1990 did not shatter the confidence of the investment community: 690,000 shares were sold at $15.75 while the book value stood at $10.52. John Parker's vow to never again sell new shares below book value was sustained.

In January 1992, Bill Holmes retired. Bill had served the Company loyally since he first began work in Kankakee in 1956. Along with Bill Evans, he was the first subsidiary manager to be named President. He was also the only subsidiary employee ever to be elected to Consumers' board. When he retired, Bill was in line to be President of the National Association of Water Companies. Accordingly, he retained an office in Portland and served in that capacity from October of that year to October 1993. Consumers had always done its share for NAWC and since 1966 had consistently had a representative on the NAWC Executive Committee. John Russell was headed for its presidency when he resigned, John White served as its President in 1972, and in 1984, John Parker served as President.

Bill was replaced by Paul D. Schumann. Paul had started working for Garden State Water Company during the summers while he was still in college. As soon as he graduated, he went to work full time, and when he succeeded Jerry Lamprey as President in 1979, he was less than thirty years old and, with the possible exception of family owned companies, probably the youngest water utility president in the country. Paul had moved to Portland in 1987 to become a Senior Vice President responsible for the Enterprise Group.

In December 1991, John Parker announced his plans to take early retirement on his sixty-second birthday in August the next year. The board had encouraged him to do so, and he had readily agreed. As he would later commiserate with several of the directors, allowing his staff to persuade him to proceed with the Sugarloaf Mountain investments was his biggest mistake with the Company. "My gut feeling was that it was not the right thing for Consumers, but they kept pounding me with the numbers and

I eventually accepted their projections." In response, those same directors expressed similar sentiments. In essence, they would reply, "We had the same gut feeling, but everything you or John White ever presented us turned out at least as well as projected. With a track record like that, how could we turn you down?" Sugarloaf was what brought down the house of cards. Had Dartmouth continued the policies followed by John Russell and Curt Scribner, the 1988-90 real estate crash would not have been a problem. The Dartmouth episode, combined with the Southern New Hampshire write-off, shattered the board's confidence. But, fortunately, the Company had rebounded and was in excellent shape for a successor President.

In spite of the Dartmouth loss, the company had progressed during the eight years of John Parker's watch. The Company increased its customer base by over 30% and net plant by over 100%. Revenues increased 48% and, in 1991, net income was 84% higher than 1983. Even on a per share basis, the numbers were favorable. After adjustment for another 2 for 1 stock split in 1986, earnings from operations were up 24%, total earnings 40%, and book value per share 30%. Dividends per share increased 85% while the payout ratio in 1991 was 64%. That number was helped by the Marysville sale, but even against earnings before such gains, the payout was less than 80% and below the industry average.

CHAPTER ELEVEN

New Blood and the End of the Line

There were two or three people within the Company who had experience and skills comparable to that of Consumers' previous Presidents when they took over the helm, but the board was anxious to explore other options. A headhunting firm was engaged and, for the first time in the Company's history, there was an outside search for a new President. Two or three candidates came from other investor-owned water utilities, but none of them had any more to offer than the internal candidates.

One candidate easily rose to the top of the list. That was Peter L. Haynes, most of whose career had been in the telephone industry. Most recently, he had been President and Chief Executive Officer of NYNEX Enterprises, a NYNEX subsidiary that served as a supplier for NYNEX's operating phone companies. It was a much bigger operation than

Consumers with 2,100 employees and over a billion dollars in sales. When it was operating, it had to compete with independent suppliers, but it was designed to be a profit center for NYNEX. It was highly efficient and captured most of the supply business for NYNEX. Unfortunately for NYNEX's telephone customers, the New York Public Service Commission took the position that NYNEX Enterprises was merely a department of NYNEX and, as with every other utility, such departments are to be operated on a

Peter L. Haynes, Consumers' president when the Company merged with Philadelphia Suburban Corporation

cost basis with no allowance for profit. Little wonder that NYNEX eventually decided to liquidate the company and invest its money elsewhere. With an entrepreneurial spirit, Peter was in the process of setting up a similar company with some venture capital partners when the Consumers opportunity came along. He elected to take the safer course. A Maine native, Peter held an engineering degree from the University of Maine and an MBA from Cornell. The Consumers job offered him an opportunity to return to the state he loved. John White reports that around the time Peter was going to college in Orono, John, attending to the business of recently acquired Camden and Rockland Water Company, would occasionally meet with Peter's father who was serving as Manager of the city of Rockland. Peter was a bit apprehensive that running a water company might be boring, and came aboard with the understanding that he might well serve for only five years. As it turned out, Peter acknowledges that it was a refreshing challenge, and served for almost seven full years, to the very end.

Peter was a big breath of fresh air. Having served in the telephone industry, he was totally familiar with the regulatory process, and he brought to the Company new systems and ideas that he had gained from twenty-seven years in the telephone industry. Among other things, he introduced a service-oriented quality process throughout the Company and established a marketing program that included a revised corporate identity.

It didn't take long for Peter to learn the water business. The recovery of water utility earnings continued in 1992 and, in fact, all the way through 1995 with increases to record highs each year. The Enterprise Group, however, continued to be a challenge. C/P extended its Merrill Creek contract for another five years, secured contracts totaling $8 million to install meters in New York City and opened an office in Orlando, Florida, in anticipation of numerous opportunities in that state. C/P was actually the largest third party installer of water meters in the country. The meter contracts generated a lot of money but, because of the competitive environment, the margins were very thin. In 1992 C/P had a good year and appeared to be most promising. Burlington, however, suffered another loss and, hoping for a turnaround, Peter hired a new President for that subsidiary.

Near the end of 1992, the Company bought from General Water Works the water utilities in **Greenville**, **Skowhegan** and **Millinocket**, Maine. Several years earlier, General had become so discouraged with the rate regulation in Maine that it had initiated a program to dispose of all its Maine holdings. Several of the properties were sold to their respective municipalities, but for five properties, the local governments had no interest. Thus, the above three were sold to Consumers at an attractive price.

Bill Holmes and John Parker did not stand for re-election to the board in 1993. For years, John had been fielding questions at the annual shareholders' meeting as to why there were no women on Consumers' board. With two vacancies, the board decided to do something about it. J. Bonnie Newman, a successful businesswoman in southern New Hampshire. and Elaine D. Rosen, a Senior Vice President at UNUM, the large insurance company headquartered in Portland, were elected to fill their seats. In the same spirit, Judy Hayes was appointed President of Consumers' three Maine water companies which operated eight separate utilities. Judy is the daughter of Otto Wallingford, the well-known developer of Lost Valley ski area in Auburn and inventor of sophisticated snowgrooming equipment that is a market leader worldwide. Judy had joined Consumers right after graduating from Bowdoin and had quickly risen through the ranks on the financial side of the business. Two years later, another woman, Sharon Schulman, was appointed President of all of Consumers' New Jersey operations.

1993 was also a year of extensive financing. Another 690,000 common shares were sold, again on favorable terms, i.e., net to the Company $16.71 vs. a book value of about $12 per share. Once again, Tucker Anthony, Inc., headed up the underwriting. The Company also took advantage of some changes in the tax law whereby, with the cooperation of the municipalities involved, the subsidiaries could issue tax-exempt bonds. Some $30 million were issued on that basis, of which $12 million was refinancing existing debt.

But problems still existed in the Enterprise Group. Turning around Burlington was not to be, and in the fall the Company announced that the business was for sale. From 1991 through 1993, Burlington lost a total of $1.6 million and, on announcing the sale, a reserve for an additional $5.3 million loss, net of taxes, was booked. In July 1994, the company was sold for $378,000, a fraction of what Consumers paid for the business eleven years earlier.

Offsetting part of those losses was the sale of Ohio's Washington Court House Division under the threat of condemnation for $10 million with a gain, net of taxes, of $3 million. The next year, the Company's Damariscotta, Maine, system was sold for $1.5 million with a gain after taxes of $363,000. In that time period, small portions of several other systems were also taken over by local municipalities.

The late 1980's and the '90's brought on the largest capital budgets in the history of the Company. The bulk of the expenditures were forced by the Safe Drinking Water Act. Nine of the Company's fourteen water treatment plants were either built, rebuilt, or extensively refurbished. That, of course, precipitated record levels of financing and, in turn, record levels of rate case activity. The capital construction peaked at over $35 million in 1995 and thereafter tapered down to more normal levels.

As Peter Haynes expressed it in his Annual Letter to Shareholders for 1996, Consumers that year was a victim of Murphy's Law. Because of the rainiest summer on record, utility earnings were down and, on top of that, Consumers was on the losing end of two decisions, one involving a suit against a contractor for one of Ohio's Treatment Plants and the other the treatment of a sale of land in Illinois. (Subsequently, the latter decision was reversed after appeal by the Company.) Of greater impact was a desperate attempt to salvage C/P through a restructuring that required a write-off of $2.4 million. The bottom line was net earnings per share of $.72 compared to $1.34 the year before.

But the next year, as Peter wrote to the shareholders, "Murphy has gone on to bother someone else." Water utility earnings were the best in the Company's history, capital expenditures were down, and the Company benefited from several small acquisitions and new operating contracts.

The strong results were offset, however, by another major write-off. As with Burlington, there was no turnaround for C/P. Before year-end, it was announced that Consumers would liquidate the company. In anticipation of the process, a reserve of $2.35 million was booked. Excluding the $2.4 write-off of the previous year, C/P had lost over $1.8 million during the years 1995 through 1997. With the liquidation of C/P, for the first time since 1930, Consumers had nothing on its plate but its own water utilities and a few water utility operating contracts. Most likely, John McInnes, who had died in December 1992, was calling down, "I told you there were sharks out there." It is painful to think how different matters would have been had the Company sold Dartmouth, Arcadia, Burlington, and C/P the same year it sold Schiavi Homes. But hindsight is always so easy.

In the year that Murphy visited, 1996, there was another tragedy. Claudio Elia, CG's representative on Consumers' board, was on the plane that was flying into Bosnia with a team of experts to assess various means to assist that war-torn country in reconstruction. The crash was well publicized in the national press. Michel Avenas was nominated by CG (renamed Vivendi) to take Claudio's place.

And there were other board changes. Earlier, in 1993, Eliot Payson did not stand for re-election because of the age restriction. Eliot had been a valuable contributor for thirty-three years and for the first time in the Company's history, there was no Payson on Consumers' board. In 1996, because of the Company's age restriction, John White did not stand for re-election. From his first employment to his retirement as a director, John had been associated with Consumers for fifty years, by far the longest of anybody. There is no need to repeat here his accomplishments. Robert O. Viets, President and CEO of Cilcorp, Inc., an energy services business in Illinois, was elected to take his place. In 1997 Dave Hastings did not stand for board re-election, again because of the age policy. Dave had served on the board thirty-three years, including twelve years as its Chairman. Dave had been a wonderful chairman. From that experience, the writer feels strongly that corporate governance is wrong when a company's CEO is also designated Chairman of the board. A board of directors is supposed to represent the interests of a company's shareholders and there's always a risk that a CEO chairman is more interested in his own career than the welfare of the shareholders. A CEO president has all the authority necessary to run a company and should have someone to whom he reports. Absent an independent chairman, by default, too many CEOs report to no one but themselves while the independent directors have no rallying point in case of concerns. For a case in point, compare, if you will, the awkward maneuvers to bring in Harold Payson as President when Vernon West was serving as both President and chairman (without title) with the smooth transition from John Parker to Peter Haynes. Given the success of Dave Hastings' chairmanship, the board elected John Menario to

David R. Hastings II, left, and John E. Menario, right,
Consumers' two "independent" chairmen.

succeed him. The last change in Consumers' board was the
decision by Bill Russell in 1998 not to stand for re-election.
Bill had ably and faithfully been a great addition to board
deliberations for twenty-eight years.

In 1997 the board retained Lockridge & Co. to give
advice as to alternative strategies and ways to improve
shareholder value. Lockridge's report applauded many of
the cost-saving measures that the Company had instituted
on its own, including the establishment of a central financial services center in Ohio. For years, Consumers' parent
company financial center had been in Portland while the
primary data processing had been located in Boardman,
Ohio. The data processing was headed up by Consumers'
Vice President for Information Services, Jerry D. Snellen.
Jerry was one of the best, if not the best, such officer in the
water utility industry and survived the eventual merger
with Philadelphia Suburban to assume the same responsibility for the combined company. Lockridge had several

recommendations, including a new approach for allocating capital and better techniques for identifying and assessing potential acquisitions.

Privately owned water utilities as large as Roaring Creek or Inter-State were almost non-existent by 1997. There were still a few small operations that might be acquired, but unless they were close enough to an existing system and could, therefore, be inter-connected or operated as a satellite, most were not an attractive target. In 1996, Consumers did purchase the **Hartland** and **Bucksport** systems in Maine because they fit well with the modus operandi of Consumers Maine Water Company which was operating eight widely separated water utilities. The Hartland situation was another feather in Consumers' hat. The Hartland and Waldoboro water utilities had been owned by General Water Works and were the two companies that Consumers did not get when General sold its last five Maine properties. But the individual who purchased them did not manage them well, and when the service became intolerable, the Maine PUC turned to Consumers Maine Water Company to salvage the situation. The outcome was that Consumers bought Hartland and secured a contract to operate Waldoboro, which the town elected to purchase. The Bucksport Water Company was purchased from Champion Paper Company. Fifty years earlier, that mill, with its water utility, was controlled by New England Public Service Company whose President was one of Consumers' founding directors, William B. Skelton.

The industry had matured, and for any company as large as Consumers to grow significantly, the only avenue was to merge with or acquire one of the large publicly traded water utility companies. By 1997, there were still seventeen such companies, but a consolidation was gaining momentum. In 1994, United Water Resources, whose primary water utility was Hackensack Water Company, purchased General Water Works. Overnight, that made United a multi-state water utility holding company. In mid-1997, a major water company attempted to purchase Consumers. Because of that and the Lockridge report, Consumers retained SG Barr Devlin to offer advice concerning both the acquisition initiative and its own acquisition program. Utilizing Barr Devlin's advice, Consumers refrained from entering into discussions with that water company.

Shortly thereafter, however, Nicholas DeBenedictis, Chairman, President and CEO of Philadelphia Suburban Corporation, the holding company of Philadelphia Suburban Water Company and several nearby water utilities, approached Peter Haynes and opened up a dialogue concerning a possible merger. There were no specifics discussed, but both Presidents advised their boards of the conversation. In March 1998, Mr. DeBenedictis called John Menario and, at a meeting between the two on April 7 and 8, they determined that there were sufficient reasons for continued discussions. By then, PSC had Salomon Smith Barney engaged as its consultant, and in May there were meetings, both between Salomon Smith Barney and Barr Devlin, and between Nick DeBenedictis and Peter Haynes along with their chief financial officers, Michael P. Graham and John Isacke. The dialogues and exchanges of information accelerated, and immediately following special board meetings in June, on Saturday, June 27, 1998, a merger agreement was executed. The agreement was announced publicly before the market opened on Monday.

The agreement called for an exchange of stock whereby Consumers would become a subsidiary of PSC. On a total capitalization basis, PSC was approximately 50%

larger than Consumers. The basic exchange ratio equated to Consumers shareholders receiving $30 of PSC stock for each share of Consumers stock. It was recognized, however, that between June 27 and the date of closing there were several time-consuming hurdles to cross, and during that interim, the stock prices of both companies could change considerably. Thus, a so-called "collar" was placed around the exchange ratio whereby, if the price of PSC stock increased, the maximum exchange consideration would be $32 while, if PSC's stock decreased, the minimum exchange consideration would be $28. There were numerous other provisions, but the primary hurdles were approval by the shareholders of both companies and approval by all the state public utility commissions involved.

The prospecti issued to the respective shareholders outlined the advantages to each company and included assertions by both Barr Devlin and Salomon Smith Barney that the deal was fair for both parties. From 1990 through 1997, Consumers' stock price had varied between a low of $10 per share (in 1990) and a high of $21.25 (in 1993). The most common price during that period was around $18 per share. In 1998, Consumers' stock began to creep up, and on the last trading day before the announcement of the deal, it reached $24.25 per share. The author suspects that, as is normal, it is impossible to totally conceal discussions between corporations and, as the announcement approached, an excess of buyers pushed up the stock price.

Within the Consumers' family, there were very mixed emotions. Among the employees, there was understandable apprehension. For most shareholders, the deal was attractive since their stock had gone virtually nowhere in ten years. Nevertheless, since Consumers' dividend per share was significantly higher than PSC's, even with the premium exchange, dividends for the Consumers' shareholders would decrease slightly. Shareholders and retirees in Maine mourned the loss of a significant Maine institution. For years, Consumers had been one of only a handful of publicly traded corporations both incorporated and headquartered in Maine and doing the bulk of its business outside the state. Further, while both the Company and its employees donated and rendered service to charitable causes in all the areas served, for years Consumers, the Parent, had been a generous supporter of numerous institutions in the Greater Portland area. Now that support would come to a screeching halt with the closure of Consumers' corporate headquarters. A long-loved and respected Maine institution would cease to exist.

The shareholder approvals were gained with overwhelming majorities. The stock prices did fluctuate with Consumers stock taking a predictable jump following the announcement and PSC stock enjoying an unexplained significant rise. Absent the collar, there were periods when Consumers stock would have equated to over $40 per share based on the basic exchange ratio and the price of PSC stock. The public utility commissions in typical style were slow in responding to the petitions for approval. Ultimately, all the states approved the transaction, and on March 10, 1999, the merger was completed. Whereas the original agreement anticipated an exchange ratio of 1.459 shares of PSC for each share of Consumers, the ultimate exchange was 1.432 shares of PSC worth $32 per Consumers share. Only two weeks after its seventy-third birthday the control of Consumers Water Company moved from Portland, Maine, to Bryn Mawr, Pennsylvania, on the so-called Pennsylvania Main Line.

CHAPTER TWELVE

Epilogue

Consumers went out flying high. The Company's results for 1998 were never distributed to the shareholders because they were not available before the closing. Consumers earned more in 1998 than in any year of its history. Earnings per share were $1.80, beating for the first and only time, after adjustment for stock splits and stock dividends, the $17.55 EPS of the year Springfield was sold. Earnings for 1998 were helped by the involuntary sale of Consumers New Hampshire Water Company to the Town of Hudson. That sale generated a gain of $3.9 million, the largest such gain in the history of the Company including the sale of Springfield,[7] or $0.43 per share. Nevertheless, earnings per share from operations alone were also at an all-time high with the exception of 1987 and 1988 which benefited from strong earnings from the Enterprise Group.

---

[7] The financial impact of the New Hampshire sale was, of course, nowhere near as significant as the Springfield sale since (1) in 1998 the Company was much larger and (2) the dollars gained have not been adjusted for inflation since 1957.

Peter Haynes had made a valiant effort to salvage Burlington and C/P, but it wasn't in the cards. Stripped of all its diversification, the Company was stronger than ever. Under Peter's seven years of guidance, in spite of the loss of Washington Court House, Southern New Hampshire, Damariscotta, Burlington and C/P, the Company had grown. The number of water customers netted out to about the same, but because of the heavy capital improvement program, net utility plant increased over $100 million or a little over 35%. Reflecting that investment, gross revenue increased almost 17% despite the large revenue loss with the demise of Burlington and C/P. More important, during the same period earnings per share from operations increased almost 20%, and the record of annually increasing dividends to shareholders remained intact.

Consumers' corporate headquarters were closed less than a month after the exchange. Most of the officers and other employees, some fifteen in all, loyally stayed on the job until the end. With a robust economy, virtually all the hourly employees found new employment in short order. Peter Haynes retired but remained almost fully occupied as National Chairman of the Boys and Girls Clubs of America. Most of the other Portland officers were offered comparable positions in Philadelphia, but, although not one was a native, they all elected to stay in the state of Maine. Most of them, too, quickly found new employment. As already stated, Jerry Snellen, who was a corporate officer located in Boardman, Ohio, did assume responsibility for PSC's management information system. Bob Ervin, Consumers' Vice President and Treasurer who transferred to Boardman when the Company's financial center was moved, was still on the job as this was written. In addition, four of Consumers' directors went on the board of PSC, namely,

Michel Avenas, John Menario, John Palmer, and Robert Viets. Robert G. Liptak who had been President of Consumers' Pennsylvania companies since 1982, was appointed President of Consumers Water Company reporting to Nick DeBenedictis. Reporting to Bob are the other four state presidents, Judy Hayes of Consumers Maine Water Company, Walter J. (Buzz) Pishkur of Consumers Ohio Water Company, Terry J. Rakocy of Consumers Illinois Water Company, and Sharon E. Shulman of Consumers New Jersey Water Company. Responsibility for Consumers' Pennsylvania properties was divided. Buzz Pishkur assumed responsibility for Shenango Valley while the eastern properties were picked up

John White holding a Consumers stock certificate he keeps framed in his home office. The certificate was given to him by Vernon West in 1948, and when it was exchanged for PSC stock 51 years later John figures that, after adjustment for stock dividends and splits, its value had appreciated approximately 165 times over.

by PSC's Pennsylvania operations. For the vast majority of Consumers' six-hundred-odd high-quality, skilled, and loyal employees, little has changed.

PSC purchased a first-class company. At all levels the Company had excellent employees. The massive capital expenditures to meet the requirements of the Safe Drinking Water Act and anticipated growth were essentially complete, and all the systems and operations were on the cutting edge. Consumers' shareholders benefited from a premium price, but PSC by no means overpaid. The premium was par for the course in a period of rapid consolidation of the industry. In 1990 there were eighteen publicly traded water companies. By the end of the decade, eight had either been sold or were under contract. By purchasing Consumers, PSC firmly positioned itself as second largest independent in the industry. Except for American, the remaining publicly traded water companies are significantly smaller.

TABLES

CONSUMERS PRESIDENTS (OR CEO CHAIRMAN)

Vernon F. West	1926–1951	John W. L. White	1966–1984
Harold C. Payson	1951–1957	John van C. Parker	1984–1992
Fletcher W. Means	1957–1966	Peter L. Haynes	1992–1999

CONSUMERS VICE PRESIDENTS

Harold C. Payson	1926–1951	John F. Isacke	1983–1999
Fletcher W. Means	1951–1957	Robert W. Phelps	1983–1990
Richard N. Berry	1956–1957	Brian R. Mullany	1986–1999
John J. Russell	1958–1969	Paul D. Schumann	1987–1999
John W. L. White	1962–1966	Jerry D. Snellen	1987–1999
Peter N. Johnson	1968–1979	Judith W. Hayes	1989–1993
John van C. Parker	1968–1984	Stanley R. Goodnow	1992–1993
Paul F. Noran	1979–1999	Robert E. Ervin	1993–1999
William D. Holmes	1982–1992		

PRIMARY STAFF OFFICERS[*]

SECRETARY
James W. Coburn 1926–1956
John W. L. White 1957–1965
Daniel T. C. Drummond 1966
John van C. Parker 1967–1975
Morris E. Bailey 1976–1977
Brian R. Mullany 1978–1999

CHIEF ENGINEER
Herman Burgi 1926–1948
John W. L. White 1949–1956
Harry Wooster 1957
Gerald H. Lamprey 1958–1964
Peter N. Johnson 1965–1978
Paul F. Noran 1979–1999

CHIEF FINANCIAL OFFICER
James W. Coburn 1926–1956
John W. L. White 1957–1965
John J. Russell 1966–1968
John van C. Parker 1969
Gordon F. LaBay 1970–1975
John van C. Parker 1976–1978
Robert W. Phelps 1979–1989
John F. Isacke 1990–1999

---

[*] The actual titles varied from year to year, but the responsibility assigned was essentially the same.

RESIDENT PRESIDENTS OF MAJOR SUBSIDIARIES*

Consumers Illinois Water Company
William D. Holmes 1965–1984
Charles H. Smith 1985–1996
Terry J. Rakocy 1996–1999

Consumers Pennsylvania Water Co.
William T. Evans 1965–1981
Robert G. Liptak, Jr. 1982–1999

Consumers New Jersey Water Co.
John Exley 1969–1970
Gerald H. Lamprey 1973–1978
Paul D. Schumann 1979–1988
Elmer E. Martin 1988–1991
Ronald F. Williams 1991–1994
Sharon E. Schulman 1995–1999

Consumers Maine Water Company
Robert H. Varney 1969–1982
Kenneth P. Jacobson 1983–1993
Judith W. Hayes 1993–1999

Consumers Ohio Water Company
Pierce Bailey 1973–1980
Wallace E. DeArment 1980–1992
Walter J. Pishkur 1992–1999

Southern New Hampshire Water Company
J. Michael Love 1987–1990
Robert W. Phelps 1990–1994
Terry J. Rakocy 1994–1996

The Dartmouth Company
Curtis M. Scribner 1974–1982
F. Gordon Hamlin 1982–1989
Stanley R. Goodnow 1990–1991

Burlington Homes of New England
Edward J. Keiser 1983–1986
John H. Ireton-Hewett 1987–1992
Charles R. Wood 1992–1994

Schiavi Homes
John H. Schiavi 1983–1985
John L. Palmer 1985–1986

C/P Utility Services
Bradley E. Taylor 1987–1995
James P. Laurito 1996

Arcadia Company
Paul S. Laughlin 1983
Stanley R. Goodnow 1986–1991

---

* Over the years the names of the subsidiaries have changed, but for this table the most recent name has been utilized.

CONSUMERS DIRECTORS

NAME	YEARS SERVED		NUMBER OF YEARS SERVED
George F. West	1926–1943		17
Vernon F. West	1926–1963		37 Including 6 years as Chairman
Herbert Payson	1926–1930		4
Harold C. Payson	1926–1963		37
William B. Skelton	1926–1932	1951–1964	19
Philip Burgess	1926–1955		29
James W. Coburn	1926–1957		31
Phillips M. Payson	1930–1960		30
Thomas M. Huston	1932–1942		10
Arthur N. Burnie	1943–1946		3
John McInnes	1944–1988		44 Including 12 years Advisory
Fletcher W. Means	1946–1970		34 Including 4 years as Chairman
Albert L. Sylvester	1955–1958		3
J. Albert M. Thomas	1955–1958		3
Richard N. Berry	1957–1958		1
Howard Butcher III	1958–1959		1
W. Frederick Spence	1958–1959		1
John J. Russell	1958–1969	1976–1990	25
John W. L. White	1958–1996		38 Including 3 years as Chairman
George S. Payson	1959–1977		18
Eliot B. Payson	1960–1994		34
Benjamin R. Alexander	1963–1979		16 Including 5 years Advisory
David R. Hastings	1963–1997		34 Including 13 years as Chairman
William L. Skelton	1964–1967		3
Albert F. Hauptfuhrer	1965–1971		6
William B. Skelton II	1967–1977		10
William B. Russell	1970–1998		28
John van C. Parker	1971–1993		22
Pierce Bailey	1973–1980		7
G. Taylor Evans	1973–1981		8 Including 7 years Advisory
James E. Mitchell	1973–1990		17 Including 10 years Advisory
Jack S. Ketchum	1978–1999		21
John E. Palmer, Jr.	1978–1999		21

John E. Menario	1980–1999	19 Including 2 Years as Chairman
Richard B. Ryon	1983–1989	6
John H. Schiavi	1983–1999	16
William D. Holmes	1984–1993	9
Jean–Claude Banon	1987–1990	3
Claudio Elia	1990–1995	5
Peter L. Haynes	1992–1999	7
Jane E. Newman	1993–1999	6
Elaine D. Rosen	1993–1997	4
Michel Avenas	1997–1999	2
Robert O. Viets	1997–1999	2

UTILITIES AND BUSINESSES OWNED BY CONSUMERS WATER COMPANY*

WATER UTILITIES

Illinois

Kankakee Water	1926–1999
University Park	1984–1999
Inter–State Water	1986–1999
Woodhaven	1987–1999
Candlewick	1988–1999
Oak Run	1989–1999

Maine

Penobscot County Water	1926–1928
York Shore Water	1928–1930
Freeport Water	1930–1999
Winterport Water	1930–1970
Camden and Rockland Water	1959–1999
Newport Water	1962–1980
Wilton Water	1963–1983
Wiscasset Water	1964–1984
Damariscotta Water	1964–1995
Oakland Water	1968–1999
Kezar Falls Water	1971–1999

Maine (continued)

Skowhegan Water	1992–1999
Millinocket Water	1992–1999
Greenville Water	1992–1999
Bucksport Water	1996–1999
Hartland Water	1996–1999

Missouri

Springfield City Water	1930–1957

Nebraska

Plattsmouth Water	1928–1943

New Hampshire

Hudson Water	1930–1998

New Jersey

Blackwood Water	1964–1999
Hamilton Square Water	1965–1999
Peoples Water	1968–1999

New York

Wanakah Water	1965–1990

* Excludes small satellites operated by larger systems and utilizes name first used by Consumers.

Ohio

Delaware Water	1926–1936
Masury Water	1926–1999
Massillon Div., OWS	1973–1999
Lake Erie West Div., OWS	1973–1999
Lake Erie East Div., OWS	1973–1999
Struthers Division, OWS	1973–1999
Marysville Division, OWS	1973–1991
Washington Court House Div., OWS	1973–1994
Mahoning Valley Div., OWS	1973–1999

Pennsylvania

Shenango Valley Water	1926–1999
Beaver Valley Water	1926–1940
Williamsport Water	1927–1929
Sayre Water	1968–1999
Erie Suburban Water	1969–1985
Roaring Creek Water	1985–1999

Virginia

Roanoke Water Works	1931–1938

NON-UTILITIES

Dartmouth Real Estate	1930–1991
Schiavi Homes	1983–1986
Burlington Homes	1983–1994
Arcadia Company	1983–1991
C/P Utility Services	1983–1998

INDEX

	DATE DUE	
DEC 1 7 2001		